Before meeting Christa and subsequently being given the honor of editing this invaluable life tool you now hold in your hands, my life had become chaotic and was heading down a path I didn't want. As a wife, a homeschooling mom of 8 kids all still living at home, and running a successful business from my home, my priorities were turned completely upside down. I was following what many "experts" sell as the recipe for success: sacrifice 2-4 years of my life and time with my family and that would lead to freedom and success. But the more I struggled to follow that recipe as I continued to climb the success ladder, all I was finding was even greater stress, more striving in my own power, more chaos, more overwhelm, and I became somewhat resentful at times of the business I started that I once used to LOVE and had been so passionate about. This was definitely NOT the successful OR harmonious life I desperately desired for myself and my family.

After beginning to implement the priorities as Christa offers here, the first several days I jumped out of bed hours before my alarm, and my kids, many of whom are really early risers, said, "Mom! You're up early! Are you going somewhere?" That was both an "Ouch!" and a "Wow!" moment. My kids started noticing and loving the changes in me immediately! My hubby did too, and I'll just leave it at that.

With my priorities now in order, doing what I was DESIGNED to do, not what I THOUGHT I was supposed to be doing, instead of dreading my alarm and getting out of bed every day, I'm now EXCITED to start my day and my productivity has skyrocketed! My kids have their mom back, my husband has his wife back, and projects around our home that had been piling up for a really long time are

now getting done, which just encourages me to keep up this new way of living even more. Life is SO much easier and flows SO much more smoothly when you get your priorities straight.

I cannot recommend this book highly enough to any wife and/or mom who is struggling day-to-day, maybe who feels she's lost her way, or she's lost her identity, and feels that there's just GOT to be something more than the rat race she currently finds herself in. If that describes you, this book is for you, Sweet Friend.

Come on in, grab a cup of tea, get comfy, and dive in. Give yourself permission to discover, not what the WORLD says you should be, but who you were DESIGNED to be. Welcome Home, Beautiful! ♥

Carrie Solorzano

Wow! I am honored to read this, thank you! Working to create a home full of peace and harmony, one in which each person feels honored and cared for, felt just plain impossible. I literally felt like I was swirling in a cave of confusion. Where do I even start?

Reading this literally flipped a switch in my brain, setting me into a more focused mindset reminding me I have NO time to waste! Each page is full of my own notes on her teachings.

Christa's transparent honesty and practical, easy-to-implement strategies have given me tunnel vision for finding joy and thriving first in my home, then in my relationships and business. Her relevant stories and real-life examples have proven to me that it is indeed simple to CHOOSE to speak life, call out greatness in my family, find extreme focus, be faithful with the little, simplify, surrender my desires and plans, and even find favor in a home-based business.

I am now excited about my role as wife and mom more than any other role I could ever have! *This anointed writing literally sealed the deal for me and answered the lingering question in my mind, "Do I really want to homeschool our boys?" YES! So... homeschooling begins Monday!*

I will be gifting this book to new moms and sharing it with every woman I know!

Angela

Today is your day. A new beginning. An awakening of sorts.

As you read Christa's heart, beautifully written like having a conversation with her in her home, you'll be empowered, feel loved and seen, and you'll taste hope. Her wins and her mistakes are woven throughout — a combo of magical realism and delight. You won't want to put this book down because somehow, in some way, she relates to every kind of person.

If you want change in your life you'll eat this book up and have it for dessert. If you're satisfied with where you are in every area, it's not for you. You may not even know what you need. But my guess is there will be a hundred nuggets you can implement — the day you read it. I'm a fan of learning from successful people.

Christa's successes are borne from pain and humility, and sweet reality. As she exposes her heart and secrets, your own pain may be exposed. I promise if you stare it in the face, you will be able to do what she's done — success in your home and personal life, and then your unique beauty and success will shine in every other area of life.

I love you, Christa! Thank you for the ways you see me. I'm glad the rest of the world can now be seen by you.

Sandi Weldon Boudreau

Live Beautiful

7 Secrets to Building your Business & Family Without Regrets

Contents

Dedication

With a heart to give honor to whom it is due, I dedicate this book to the thousands of mommies who have picked up their mantle and are choosing to prosper in it, realizing that the title of "mom" is the most important ever.

There is an emerging movement of mommies who see how important and fun this journey can be. With God behind us and the Holy Spirit in front of us, we can make a huge difference today. These moms and wives and women are turning the world upside down. Ready or not, here come our super-heroes!!

I dedicate this book to all the very important friends and family who told me I could do this. To open my heart, my life, and my secrets to share with you!! To exchange all the pain and trials for light that makes a difference.

To Bethany Puccio and family, without your steadfast love, I could never have made it.

To McKinsey Smith, my right-hand lady who makes me laugh and who spent hours brainstorming and trouble-shooting and growing as we share with you our Smith Family secrets.

To Trina Holden who spent hours with me and your incredible husband Jeremy who is the mastermind producer of this book.

To Carrie Solorzano who spent hours on the phone with me and spent many nights till wee in the morning tweaking and editing to get this into your hands!!

To Summer Cacciagioni, all your input, dear friend, and picking my brain to pull out my secrets that I do so automatically.

To Chad Ketcher who's made life so fun!

To Pam and Mark Holden who helped clean one day in the midst of all the chaos and fed our family. There is special treasure in Heaven for you, my friends!!

To my very best friend in the world, Jason Smith, my husband who has allowed me to test my greatest weaknesses and strengths on him!! You are our protector and provider, a one-of-a-kind, and there aren't enough words to say how incredibly grateful I am to call you "husband," "best friend," and "father" of our children.

9

To my beautiful children who are Nation-changers: Madison, McKinsey, Morgan, Macy, Marissa, Marti, Matthew, Michael, Meg, Melanie, Marshall, Malachi, Miracle, Manning, and Malloree. This book has been written for you and really by you. Thank you for letting me be your mom. All the great things I do and all my weaknesses. I am seriously so thankful I get to share life with you!! I am blessed.

A NOTE FROM CHRISTA...

Do you like shoes?

How many pairs do you put on during the day?

Let's take a look in your closet. We get to wear the pair of:

- The flirtatious, adoring wife
- The wise, kind mother
- The ambitious careerist
- The organized secretary
- The pristine role model
- The homework tutor
- The exotic, healthy chef
- The gym bunny
- The popular, warm friend
- The jet-setting adventurer

- The satirical fashion expert
- The put-together hair stylist/makeup artist
- The well-read intellect
- The charismatic conversationalist
- The deep, existential thinker
- The quick problem-solver
- The one who keeps up with all the news...

Stay sane.

Get your kids to practice on time WITH matching shoes... or even... shoes on... would be good.

Oh... and text people back.

Hey friend, my name is Christa Smith and I have a little experience trying to walk miles in every shoe mentioned above and I wasn't always successful.

The thing is, I had done everything by the book and I thought I had done it all right.

I married a good man, went to college, and did everything "they" tell you to do yet, ten years ago, all I had to show for it was divorce papers and food stamps cluttering my counter... Not to mention the ginormous amount of student debt asking for my spleen in compensation.

Buying a home or even going on a simple vacation didn't even make the 20-year resolution.

Even though my kids always have said and to this day still say I'm a good mom, I have felt and can still feel like a terrible mom, especially during that season.

Conventional thinking got me nowhere so I started thinking in unconventional ways, outside of the box and outside of stereotypes.

Out of desperation I made a decision that jump-started years of learning, from leadership books to educational audios from my business I turned around and applied in our home; throwing out the ones that didn't work and keeping the ones that did.

Today, I'm standing beside a hot husband of 24 years, with a cultivated million-dollar business under our belts… all the while raising and birthing 15 kids!

Making humans is no small feat in and of itself. I have been pregnant for 11.25 years in 19 years of raising children. They are an average of 14 months apart!

A feat we accomplished as much as we could

guilt-free, because we learned our family doesn't have to compete for much-needed attention while my business sweetly bloomed.

So here's the deal.

YOU are a GOOD mom.

That phrase might be hard to swallow, or even think, or say, but I know this because you took the initiative and invested money and time into your family and yourself by picking up this book and choosing a better future over the status quo that is the norm.

Congratulations!

And let me say thank you on behalf of the generations that are to come.

That shows incredible wisdom, and a trait that will be your saving grace through everything life has to offer: the ability to learn.

You are precious, an esteemed woman with a deep honor and destiny of motherhood. I know this is IN your DNA, otherwise you wouldn't be a mom. Don't listen to anything or anyone who tells you different. They are lies. Lies that could come from your own thinking pattern.

Motherhood is a queenly mantle of shaping a new generation of the world, a new nation, a new people. You are a cornerstone of this world as *"the hand that rocks the cradle rules the world."*

Maybe you have a power inside of your spirit that has been asleep. It is a power of walking in the confident woman you are made to be...

What do you say we wake it up?

After delicate work of 15 years, I've put together for you time-tested methods with proven results, backed by scientific research, to jump-start you in the right direction of that beautiful life floating in your dreams.

Be careful. These are instruments of great wealth, power, and mighty peace. If you pick them up and try them out, they will actually work whether you want them to or not.

Grab a pen, grab your notebook, jot down notes in the margins, go high-lighter happy, and enlarge the lines in your mind of what is possible; because you and I are going to cross every line in front of us and try out some gorgeous-looking new shoes on for size.

Ready to get unconventional?

I would love to stay connected with you, Beautiful Friend!

Join our WonderMom movement. We want to join hands with you here:

1) Subscribe to my YouTube Channel where I share more tips and secrets with you: "WonderMom"

2) Connect with me on Instagram: CHRISTASMITH_

3) Join our "WonderMom" Facebook group community with thousands of other like-minded friends!

4) Bookmark our website: LiveBeautifulBook.com

CHAPTER 1

A VIKING'S ARMOR

Wouldn
that could gr

Just to be
button, and
finish? A da
smiling in t
day, and sati

Well, wha
that it's more
and *tune into*

A friend of mine, who served our country in the
military, was talking with me and through him I

learned that the single most traumatized group of people in any war is not the soldiers on either side, it's not even the generals and leaders… it's the civilians; the people.

Because they either didn't know they are in a war or because they aren't prepared, organized, with no communication, they don't have the tools and they are neither on offense nor defense.

> Behind every President or world leader, like JFK or Abraham Lincoln, is a strong mother.

The first thing you must know is that this is war!

If you've ever woken up with just a brick-heavy weight on your mind and chest, weighing you down into your bed with nothing but the urge to flip over and sleep again… then you've felt a taste of the battle.

If you've ever tried to juggle all of your responsibilities, make breakfast, make sure the kids are dressed, on time, and hustling… and yet something seemingly so simple like losing a sock or your car keys seem to set you off and back five miles… then you've felt it.

Or how about when the kids have reached their limit and start to cry, in public, and you get dirty, judgmental looks… that's it.

Maybe just one thing after another boils over, falls through the cracks, and you snap out at your children, while a voice in the back of your head riddles you with bricks of guilt and shame.

Or maybe your eye catches on an adorable new-born-sized onesie but immediately a surprised and disdainful thought goes, "You can barely handle the ones you have. Who are you to neglect another kid? It'd be better if you didn't have another. You aren't the person who is equipped to handle it. You don't have enough support and you can't handle it financially."

These are just a few examples, but they are bitter tastes of a real war waged against the covenant of family.

This life, if you choose to take the red pill, is one of no regrets, seeking to forge leaders and world-shakers in your children. — *It is all out warfare* — and you are putting yourself on the front lines.

Behind every President or world leader, like JFK or Abraham Lincoln, is a strong mother.

You need armor, and you need weapons.

Every one of the secrets I share with you here are not just tips or tools. They are literal weapons I have found that effectively turn the battle in my favor.

> Music prepared the battlefield for victory for a land that was already promised them. But they still had to take it.

So let's get you fitted up with this first one—one that you should start each day with, and never go into battle without.

When the Israelites went in to capture the land that God had promised them, do you know what their battle strategy centered around?

Music.

They didn't begin fighting without it!

When they lined up for battle, the musicians were on the front line.

And we're not talking pianos or the little triangle dingy thing.

20

Horns, cymbals, and hundreds of singers made up the war path band, grounding the dust around them in song. They didn't go anywhere without them.

Music prepared the battlefield for victory for a land that was already promised them. But they still had to take it.

WHY MUSIC?

Music is a safe place!

It is a living thing that spreads to cover your mind like a protective blanket, a shield. It pulls you from your chaotic thoughts and into peace, real encouragement, and into a place that enables you to conquer.

Music pulls you into a place where you can freely conquer yourself, your position, your posture, and your mindset; it shifts the atmosphere.

When your soul agrees to the destiny gifted to you by God in song, and your eyes lift up to Him in true grateful worship, a legendary conversation happens between you and your Lord. It is a gateway to the throne room of Heaven and a bulldozer to clear out the bad day for a clean slate.

Kids love songs with hand motions. They love

using their whole body when they sing. Remember "Head, shoulders, knees, and toes?"

In Him we live and MOVE and have our being!

Music pulls you into a place where you can freely conquer yourself..., your position, your posture, and your mindset; it shifts the atmosphere.

As we get older, we get more dignified and quit using our whole body. But God made us move for a reason!

If we stomp our feet the ground will shake.

If we clap our hands the walls will break.

So what does worship look like to you? Are there certain styles of music or ways a body responds to music that you feel are not worshipful?

Do you find yourself asking what is the 'right' way to worship? Should I put my hands up high or should I put them down low? Should I put them out to the side like a cross? Should I open my eyes or keep my eyes closed?

For a comical illustration of this, go to YouTube and watch "Tim Hawkins on Hand Raising". Go ahead and watch it right now. We'll wait…

Ok! You back?

Often the worship we experience in religious culture is orderly, structured, and even solemn. When it's so routine, your mind can wander. That's when you start looking around and asking, "Are their hands up?" Having niggling concerns about what people around you are doing or thinking of you is not complete worship.

Worship *is* abandonment in all hours of every day in every place.

It's putting God in everything that you're doing and pulling your kids along with you.

It's about just you and God—no matter who else is around—kids, neighbors, friends—it shouldn't matter.

Because entering into His presence is a power move.

It's an escape into His arms and into His care; it's real trust.

King David danced naked in front of His entire

kingdom. I mean, I personally don't dance naked, but worshipping with that level of trust, joy, and abandonment that swept over King David is tasting real freedom from the coils of stress.

Powerful worship is when you are only focused on God, and you give your whole body, mind, and soul to Him in that moment. Maybe you look silly. It doesn't matter. I've had a few dance classes in my past, but that doesn't qualify me as a worshiper.

Because entering into His presence is a power move.

Worship is a chance for me to focus on a vision of this world where my day goes smoothly, and rejoicing in the God who has given this exact day to me as a love letter. Choosing joy in song and dance in harmony with your kids.

The Bible says we perish for lack of vision.

So here's what worship looks like for me. I often just wave my arms and I envision going over to people's houses bringing blessings, praying over them, and I imagine angels flying around my house and my area… even though I've never seen one, I imagine what they look like.

Turn it up

I've got news for you: *the enemy doesn't create—he imitates.*

<u>Every style</u> of music out there was originally God's.

Real worship is jumping up and down and blasting the speakers, drowning out the voices of the enemy with song and dance. It's allowing the sweet tones of commanding music to wipe clean all thoughts, save what's inside the bass-line— the heartbeat of gratefulness.

In Nehemiah we're told, "The joy of the LORD will be your strength." Our family took that promise and ran with it! We love our music LOUD and all of us like to move our bodies in wild dance as we worship the LORD.

We use drums, bells, anything that makes a noise, at a volume that reverberates through the walls, the floor, your chest, and raises your hair on end.

If it's not making the water jump in our cups, is it really loud enough?

As a musician, my husband knows speakers—but we still seem to 'blow' them regularly. We have been known to throw our unsuspecting victims into our car and record their reaction as we pumped up... I mean... turned up the volume and let them witness the Smithmobile in action.

If it's not making the water jump in our cups, is it really loud enough?

"From the lips of children and infants you, Lord, have called forth your praise." (Matthew 21:16)

Sweet Language of the Red Phone

The red phone historically was a means of communication between two world superpowers intended to decrease tensions and prevent accidental nuclear war.

Do you sometimes feel like you're on the brink of nuclear war in some area of your life? Where some area of your life has already blown up or feels like it's about to?

Pick up the red phone. The red phone is your

direct line to instant grace. It is direct access to the Maker Himself.

"But Christa," you may say. "I don't believe there is a God."

That's okay.

Some people call it "God". Some people call it "the Universe". Some people call it "Source energy".

I think that together we can agree that there is some *thing* outside of ourselves that created the world and that created us.

I encourage you to invite whoever or whatever created you to come into you now and to reveal themself to you.

So whenever you are going through a crisis, instead of turning to alcohol or drugs, or engaging in gossip which leads to word curses that the other person (like your husband) is going to have to overcome, AND you are going to have to repent of later on… That road leads to self-sabotage.

When you decide to pick up the red phone instead, you are turning your life over to God in surrender. You say, "Hey look. Here's the situation…" Tell Him what you need, with thanksgiving. Then you put the phone down and you get right back to life. And whether God fixes it or not, you CHOOSE joy and you walk in grace.

This is a strategy not exclusive to myself, but one my children have adopted when, as a mommy, you can see it written all over their face that the day didn't start out right, and I hold them and let them twirl and dance right beside me.

But I never let having kids around restrain or hinder me from living this out. They're coming along for the ride too.

It's clever to teach your children this because they are actually a secret power and there's strength in numbers!

Remember the story of Abraham asking God to spare the city his nephew was living in?

He asked God, "Will you destroy the city if there's 50 righteous people?

And God said "No".

How about 40?

"No."

He got all the way down to 10.

Ten was the number of righteousness that God required if He was to spare the city.

When I read that, I realized *10 is the legal number for a voice.*

I thought about our court system—how there must be 10 jurors in agreement for a verdict.

Ten voices can send a prisoner to jail or set them free. Use the force of numbers in your worship. Enter the courtroom of Heaven together to make your plea!

Strength to Switch

Often if I'm struggling and I feel heaviness and oppressiveness—you know that feeling when you don't know what's wrong, but you feel like there's just something in the air?

We have seen loud abandoning worship transform a dark day to one of strong productivity and harmony, as simply as switching a dark radio station to another one of beauty.

If I choose to worship in that moment—to crank it up and act out my faith, the whole atmosphere in my home shifts.

When you're in the midst of tuning in to the wrong radio station, and all that's going on in your mind are condemning dark thoughts that seem to choke you, yet you choose to praise instead—that's called a sacrifice of worship.

I love King David's example of worship throughout his life. Once he came back from a battle with his men, all their women and children had been captured and taken away. His men turned on him and were about to stone him to death.

What did he do?

He removed himself and encouraged himself in the Lord.

That's what the Psalms are. You can read the rest of the story, including a dramatic rescue, in 1 Samuel 30.

> He removed himself and encouraged himself in the Lord.

Sometimes it seems like it's almost impossible to turn to worship—it's all you can do to just turn the music on and you say, "Lord, I'm just going to listen to this song.

I'm going to say the words to the song, I'm going to just say 'Glory to Your Kingdom and Your Name.'"

It's hard. It's feeble. It's a sacrifice. But God hears and loves it when we worship.

Life is not easy. Stuff will come that will knock you to your knees.

There are things in this life we cannot or will not escape. BUT we don't need to fear, and we can ease the growing pains with the act of worship.

When you worship, you're trusting in His timing, His blessings, and His good and prosperous destiny for your life.

And when you build your life with a foundation of worship, you have all of Heaven backing you up and cheering you on. When you drive to the grocery store there are hoards of angels lining the streets shouting you on.

This is a soundtrack for success in all areas.

Turn it on.

Let it get loud.

YOUR BEAUTIFUL LIFE STARTS NOW

1) Choose what time of day you will fill your home with worship. Schedule it so it happens! Chore time is a great time to crank it up. Play worship music as you're waking up, exercising, cooking, driving, or cleaning.

2) Get a remote speaker so it's EASY to play your favorite music LOUD from any device.

3) Move the furniture and clear a space to dance to encourage your kids to worship with abandon!

CHAPTER 2

FREE SUPERPOWER

Are you a Marvel fan? Superman perhaps?

My children are fans of superheroes. For fun we like to assign superpowers around the family for impromptu story-telling.

Once my daughter mentioned she wanted the ability to warp reality. It's considered to be in the Top 5 most powerful superpowers in the fictitious hero universe.

But... what if there *were* such a thing as influence over reality?

Wouldn't that be SWEET? Think of the possibilities... You could just go crazy with it!!

Except.

There is.

The problem is that you just didn't know about it.

Until now.

WELCOME TO SECRET # 2
SPEAK LIFE.

I hardly remember my life before I learned this skill.

It was dark and shameful.

I was one of those moms who harassed her kids. And even while sharp words of condemnation, correction, and commandments left my mouth, I'd hear an equally sharp, condescending voice in my head, telling me I was a terrible failure.

I couldn't believe what came out of my mouth.

I sounded very sharp.

I had one child in particular who seemed to always push me past the limits of what was decently sane...(THE ONE WHO IS TOTALLY HELPING ME WRITE THIS BOOK.) This was when I had just 4 children.

I remember thinking, "Well, 3 out of 4 ain't bad—I just lost that kid. I don't have her heart. Oh, well." I had already given up, and it showed in how I spoke to her.

Queen of Reality?

Scripture says we will overcome by the blood of Jesus and the WORD of OUR testimony. (Revelation 12:11)

So let's take a gander and check this out. God created the universe with His words.

And then He made us in His image.

Therefore the power of life and death are IN your tongue, in the words that you speak and think.

It is a natural thing, we are His heirs; His masterpiece.

It happens whether or not we have the knowledge of it happening. That's why, uncontrolled, it can be detrimentally painful.

Honestly, when I first learned about this secret to success, I was skeptical. I had read about someone else who had cursed an almond tree and it wilted.

Could our words actually create… or kill?

I decided to test it out.

There was a bush by our mailbox that drove me nuts. It was spiny and ugly and difficult to prune, and I just wanted to get rid of it. But it was huge.

I decided to try cursing it—a great place to experiment. So, every time I drove past it or got the mail, I'd curse it. Within months this same bush got attacked by some kind of worm which ate it and it rotted away.

Gone.

It is a natural thing, we are His heirs; His masterpiece.

We didn't even have to dig up the roots. No other plant around it was affected, just the bush I'd hated and cursed.

When I finally understood about the power of the tongue and how my words were life-altering—destiny-changing…

I was mortified!

Immediately, I began to change how I spoke over my kids, and now I have made it a habit to speak life over them.

Later I found Dr. Masaru Emoto's work, "The Hidden Messages in Water." He also published several other researched books on words and how they affect water. And humans are 75% water…

An Efficient Superpower too?

One of the things I learned that changed everything for our family was the principle that *what you feed will flourish, and what you starve will die.*

When training our children, it's common to spend most of our time correcting and talking about the bad behavior, right?

But I've found that when I see something I don't like, I get way more results when I find one thing I DO like, and I speak about that!

It's a simple tactic of speaking over them what you want to see from them.

For example, with so many kids mealtimes can be chaotic!

Just imagine what it was like when I had 10 kids under 12!

I remember many times sitting at dinner and feeling so exasperated, with tension rolling through me because the table was literally moving like it was alive.

It was loud, rambunctious, and teaching manners to each individual kid simultaneously seemed like a constant tedious task.

I could have spent the whole time correcting table manners and behavior.

But what I started to do was to find one child who was doing even just a little bit of what I wanted more of, and I'd choose to focus on that.

Sometimes it was like pulling teeth to find that one little, itty, bitty thing that someone was doing right.

> But what I started to do was to find one child who was doing even just a little bit of what I wanted more of, and I'd choose to focus on that.

So first I'd pick ONE thing I wanted to see different and addressed it by saying, "Oh my gosh, look at Mira. She's sitting like a princess, she's eating with one hand, she's closing her mouth. When she eats, look at her. She's sitting up straight and she's smiling! Isn't she so pretty? Look at her!"

And then I created a game saying, "Let's everyone practice eating like a sour sally peasant!" And they would slouch over and smack. And I would ask them, "Does this look pretty? What do you see?" That created agreement which immediately saved me from the 'mean mom' image as it was their OWN idea.

Then… everyone practiced doing it the pretty way.

By edifying one child, I could affect them all!

Now I take videos and show it to them.

Suddenly they all sat up a little straighter… quieted down… and they were instantly motivated, transforming themselves into beautiful children with model manners.

By edifying one child, I could affect them all!

Not only was it effective in training behavior, but it was efficient because they were all listening at the same time, cutting down-time, and squashing the need to say the same thing over and over again.

To my boys I might say, "I love how you act like a superhero at the table! You are really powerful right now. Can I take a selfie with you?"

This is honoring and encouraging to our kids. We do this with adults, right? When you're traveling or out and about and meet someone you admire, you take a selfie with them!

Take advantage of this tool in any public venue at any given time, not just at home. This leaves a long-lasting impression of honor and respect. My kids have been incredibly blessed and have received tremendous favor because of this one thing alone.

I speak vision over them and paint a picture of what I want to see.

They're practicing being successful people, right? So I speak that over them. I'll say something like, "You know what? I'm so thankful that you guys take this time at the dinner table to practice eating like you're eating at a castle because you never know who you're going to be eating with someday. You might be eating with the President of the United States! You might travel all over the world and meet important people! I love that you're practicing right now!"

I speak vision over them and paint a picture of what I want to see.

Stick and Stones

Actual Factual Lie: Sticks and stones may break my bones, but words will never hurt me.

We shall have what we speak.

I learned this the hard way.

I once told my brother I hated him. It was one of the last conversations I had with him when we both lived at home.

I told him to leave and that life was better without him. He was joining the military and I was glad to see him go. We fought all the time.

Our relationship was never cultivated into a friendship. We never learned to speak life over each other or our relationship. We

> We shall have what we speak.

just used each other. He used me and I used him when I needed a ride.

When he came back from the Army, I was pregnant with my second child.

He had never seen a pregnant woman up close before, and he loved to see my belly. He held my child. It was the last time I saw him alive.

He took his own life later.

I just wonder if I could have asked him to forgive me.

I wonder if I could have been his teammate, could have spoken life into him, or called and asked how he was doing… I wonder if that would have a made a difference.

But my brother took his own life because he believed he didn't matter.

I had sown terrible seeds of anger and hate.

Hate is a form of murder because it means you wish they didn't exist.

I decided after the experience with my brother, that the same thing would not happen in my home. The learning from this pain with my brother would be flipped into harmony for my children. I would not allow painful speech to wreak havoc on their relationships like it did ours.

Please, don't feel sorry for me, if anything set up this story as a protective roadblock around the future of your own siblings and your children; refuse to give into any anger, hate or strife in your home, it is not welcome within your walls.

I miss him, but my brothers life is not wasted if you listen.

Order a Crop Failure

Not one of us goes unchecked with our tongue so let's order a crop failure, shall we?

If you have planted bad seeds with the words you've spoken in a relationship, it is NOT too late. The first step is to stop speaking 'bad seeds', but if you don't replace the bitterness, it's still poisoning your heart.

To clarify, you'll know when you've spoken 'bad seed' by the tiny voice that pops up and says, "You probably shouldn't have said that." If that happens, you can say, "That's not exactly what I meant…" And then say something positive and respectful. But lets

43

be real, lets repent and renounce for anything sassy that comes out of our mouth.

Its as simple as saying, "I repent, renounce and render my words powerless over you. I restore you to your natural glory inside my eyes."

"To renounce your words means to let the Lord draw off whatever you cursed. To revoke your words means to snap the spine of the curse and break it."

John Kilpatrick ~ Sid Roth interview on sidroth.org

We have to pray for the negative words already spoken to die and replace them with what we want to see in order to cancel out the future that was spoken.

You have to choose to speak the opposite.

If we say that our life sucks and our kids are monsters, we need to cancel that.

That is not who you are or who were created to be.

Speak what you want to see over

your family, and pray for God to cancel your unintended words.

Yes, you can pray for *word-crop failure.*

Ask a gracious God to negate your unintended words.

We have to pray for the negative words already spoken to die and replace them with what we want to see in order to cancel out the future that was spoken.

So, when my kids would have a sour moment, and say, "I don't wanna do piano! I hate piano! I don't wanna practice piano!" I'd say, "No, you asked for piano and God has gifted you with piano, and you need to say 10 times 'I love piano, I love piano...' To out-loud cancel what you declared."

Say *out loud* 10 things that are the opposite of the hateful or negative words you spoke.

Money Honey Bonus

Speaking life over my family gives me a decided advantage when I go out to work my business.

Why? Well, it's simple math.

You've probably heard that 93 percent of com-

munication is non-verbal. This means that body language and lifestyle speak louder than any of the words you say.

People are smart and 'hear' if you're being faithful at home. They see the stress on your head and the distracted fear pulling you back home. Especially women, who have a mother's intuition to read body language.

Body language is something you can't fake… not even the most adept actor. That's why they learn to channel real emotions and energy into their performance, otherwise it's just lying and bad acting.

This means we need to work on our non-verbal! Non-verbal body language, facial expressions, and general 'vibe' stems from your heart, thoughts, and emotions.

If you leave the house with a feeling of shame because your man is mad at you, your kids are crying, and you believe you're a failure at home, then you have to *pretend* you have it all together. But immediately your non-verbal communication gives you away and you've lost the game before you even step foot outside the door, before you ever even pick up that phone to make a call or step on stage.

People know.

Keep in mind, you're not selling a product. You're selling a way of life—another idea of living. But people don't want your stressful life! You're not selling them anything because look where it's gotten you.

SO, with that in mind, orchestrating a warm refuge in your home, an inviting escape of peace and harmony for every member of your family, is essentially the equivalent of dumping gallons of gasoline under your business… Who wants to ignite *that* fire in their business?

If your house is in order when you leave, you will have incredible power, because it is the burning fire of your unified family, your home team, pushing you forward and up.

The other day as I was headed out of the house to film a video for my WonderMom group, my 13-year old son called after me, "Go knock it out of the park, Mom!"

It didn't register at first what he had said, but I walked a few more steps and Marty who is 14 yells, "Go do a good job!"

It wasn't till I was out the door that I realized the

significance of what had just happened. A blanket of protective calmness floated over my chaotic mind. In learning to speak life over my children, I had taught them to do the same for me.

My kids were cheering me on. They were behind me, rooting for me! And I felt like I could change the world!

Because I focus on honoring them and being fully present when I'm with them, they willingly release me when it's time for me to work. There is no resentment that I am leaving. I don't have to worry that things will fall apart while I'm gone. I'm not stressed or overwhelmed… What a burden off my shoulders!

I never would have done that with my mom…

She was a nurse, but I never said to her, "Go do a good job, Mom! Go save someone's life today!" I never encouraged my mom. But my kids know the skill of speaking life and are my cheerleaders!

It's because I'm always speaking life over them, and this is the atmosphere in our home. An atmosphere I intentionally, painstakingly created over months of planting seeds of beauty… And it's worth every patient moment.

This is a secret to success—*we get more out of each other when we have encouraging teammates.*

Magnetic Influential Superpower

The title of 'wife' and 'mother' cannot be bought. They cannot be earned. They are God-given roles only. And when you are faithful with these roles, other big titles are then entrusted to your care because you are now prepared for them.

If I'm a good mom, I'm not going to give my child more if she can't handle the responsibility of what she already has. That wouldn't be in her best interest.

For instance, if she wants a car but hasn't been faithful with her room, I'm not going to give her even more responsibility and freedom. It would only hurt and overwhelm her.

But if our children are faithful, isn't it our delight to give them more?

It's the same with God.

He's given these children to me and it's my responsibility, my job in our relationship, to provide for them in every way possible to best succeed, to give them love, discernment, and encouragement.

One of the ways I do that is by constantly speaking a life of purpose over them.

Once you can master mentoring and guiding your family, God will give you more people to manage because you have been faithful with the people He has already given you.

These secret weapons are all based on the law that if you're not faithful with what you already have, then you won't be given any more. BUT, if you're faithful with a little, you'll been given much, much more.

Your spouse and your kids are your first calling and your first training ground.

If you will be faithful in using your tongue to bless and build them up, God will give you more to manage, a.k.a. business… A business has people in it—to lead.

Gossip, ingratitude, jealousy, and complaining tear apart a team, but speaking life and edifying people builds connections and calls everyone to their higher potential.

It's an essential skill for *any* type of team.

Start with the most important team in your life,

the team that will be the backbone of all your ventures. The team that no amount of division, gossip, ingratitude, or complaining can tear apart—your home team.

Superpower Applies to You

Guess who else is on your team?

You.

Speaking life over yourself and your ability to solve problems and create solutions is *crucial*.

When you face challenges, walls, difficult people, or don't know what to do next, speak life over your abilities! Speak the truth out loud. It's so simple, but so powerful!

Say 3 times a day, 5-10 times each, *out loud*, "I can do ALL things through Christ who gives me strength." Also, "Greater is HE who is IN me than HE who is IN the world."

Try it right now!

Instant Vivacious Vibe

I also teach my kids how to do this for themselves. I will declare, "God is good."

And have them repeat after me.

I have trained them to declare the truth out loud in their life. We do it all the time and it becomes a part of our family culture that swallows the friends who visit us.

They're called spoken thoughts. We are just in the business of taking our thoughts captive and bending them to our will to better our wellbeing.

I want to live life to the fullest, I want all that He has for me, and I want the same for my kids!

A simple, yet extraordinary and powerful method I've implemented into our family on a regular basis is that we love to do a family cheer when someone does something right, like showing initiative, solving a problem… any act of kindness, love, or obedience.

Whatever we want to see more of in our family, we celebrate it!

I will call out, "LeLe just went pee-pee in the potty! Everybody say, 'Go, LeLe!'" And randomly the voices of my kids will shout in unison, from all over the house, "Go, LeLe!"

I'll see Marshall pick up a piece of trash and I'll

say, "Oh my gosh, Marshall, did you just pick up that piece of trash without anyone asking you?" He'll say, "Yes," and I'll yell, "Everybody, say 'Yay Marshall!'" And it doesn't matter what everyone is doing, they'll go hoarse shouting, "Yay, Marshall! Go bud!"

At any moment in our home you may hear us break out in a cheer.

It is the affectionate atmosphere we have chosen for our home. We are focusing on what we want more of.

Harness the superpower God put in your tongue by learning the secret skill of speaking life! It is a superpower that works whether you're wielding it for good or not.

Seeing your 3-year old, in their baby accent, speak life over their older sibling because they know nothing else, says to my mom heart, "I am a good mom."

Imagine the reality of having your teenager, the one who is SUPPOSED to be moody, bratty, and hate you, INSTEAD come to you, look in your eyes and tell you, "Mom, you are a great mom and I love you."

YOUR BEAUTIFUL LIFE STARTS NOW

1) The next time you're in public and one of your kids does the tiniest thing right, surprise them by honoring them publicly. Point out what they did right and take a selfie with them!

2) Become a cheerleader in your home! When a child does something correctly, cheer loudly and invite their siblings to echo you!

3) Make it a daily habit to speak Philippians 4:13 over yourself—out loud!

CHAPTER 3

A QUEEN-LESS SOUL

Let's look at the words 'Control' and 'Influence'.

There are things you can't control, things you simply cannot anticipate. But don't be fooled. You can use your influence in a very clever yet potent way.

I once saw a movie with a man who stated a very daring line. He said, "Every woman has exactly the kind of life she wants."

Indignant, a victimized woman argued that she didn't exactly wish for the out-of-the-blue, heart-breaking events that happened in her life. He answered that this was true, but that nothing is ever 'out-of-the-blue.' She just took no responsibility in her half of the affairs and that whenever she was ready to stop crying about it, move on, and a create the beautiful life that she kept wishing for, then she would.

The reason she didn't was because she was comfortable being miserable. It was known territory.

Now it's time to come see what it's like living by the rules that you write.

SECRET # 3
YOU ARE QUEEN
OF YOUR OWN FATE

I graduated with a degree in physiology and was a sleepless, proud owner of chaotic studies up to my eyeballs whilst attending medical and nursing school when… God gave me my first child. An event I had no control over.

As I didn't have the skill-set to manage a professional career while equally juggling being a wife and mom, I realized I had complete control over a single choice.

I could either follow God in this path of family He set before me, or I could follow my career, at the sacrifice of my family.

I was unwilling to live with the regret of having

someone else raise my children. Plus I was already struggling and our finances were completely strapped.

Quitting my current job looked impossible, but I had to be willing to trust Him.

So I shelved my studies to focus on what God had given me, against all odds.

I noticed God likes to move especially when all odds are against you because when you've exhausted your own resources and intellect, then and ONLY then you'll have no doubt as to who is your saving grace. No man could receive any of the credit.

Once you make this decision, it isn't necessarily jolly to let go of your income, recognition, and community FOR the small child in front of you. All I know is that I made this same decision and we never went without a meal.

I chose to focus on my home and being the best wife and mom I could be.

My hairstylist and I were talking and she mentioned that a coach had told her never to use the term "family" because it has earned itself a bad reputation as dysfunctional and toxic, and to instead use the word "team."

Maybe it's because we have left our posts and that's why it sucks. We have traded our position as wife and mother and sold it for the hopes of wealth. Emasculating our men so that now we are the providers.

A man's greatness is in proportion to his service.

Abraham Lincoln said, "Whatever you do, put your whole mind into it. Hold it there until it is done." I knew this principle in my studies and had expounded greatly on it, but hadn't learned how to apply it in my home yet...

But once I did, my blessings swelled in abundance, in ways that were shocking, humbling, and incredible... a testament of God's might and strength. He is my advocate.

He's your advocate too, an advocate of family. Family was His idea.

A man's greatness is in proportion to his service.

I had to learn cheerful, happy service in my home and to become a great master of where I was planted.

I read about a woman and the prophet Elijah in the bible…

So he arose and went to Zarephath. And when he came to the gate of the city, indeed a widow was there gathering sticks. And he called to her and said, "Please bring me a little water in a cup, that I may drink."

And as she was going to get it, he called to her and said, "Please bring me a morsel of bread in your hand."

So she said, "As the LORD your God lives, I do not have bread, only a handful of flour in a bin, and a little oil in a jar; and see, I am gathering a couple of sticks that I may go in and prepare it for myself and my son, that we may eat it, and die."

I am gathering a couple of sticks so I can make our last meal, and then my son and I will die.

And Elijah said to her, "Do not fear; go and do as you have said, but make me a small cake from it first, and bring it to me; and afterward make some for yourself and your son.

"For thus says the LORD God of Israel: 'The bin of flour shall not be used up, nor shall the jar of oil run dry, until the day the LORD sends rain on the earth.'"

So she went away and did according to the word of Elijah; and she and he and her household ate for many days.

The bin of flour was not used up, nor did the jar of oil run dry, according to the word of the LORD which He spoke by Elijah.

I am gathering a couple of sticks so I can make our last meal, and then my son and I will die.

This story is about a woman who said the words, "We will eat our last meal and then die." That is what despair sounds like.

Yet she was still working, gathering sticks; still doing everything she could with what she had. She gave to the Lords beloved, Elijah the prophet, before herself, she served. And God blessed her.

So what do you have?

I had been given this man. This child. So, I focused on serving.

It was tedious, grueling work.

My days consisted of a perpetual torrent of endless grimy clothes, scummy dishes, running four loads of laundry and three dishwasher cycles at the very LEAST... not to mention I'd have more luck sweeping mud in the midst of a tornado than the sticky dirt that tracked through my floors daily.

I had dreams I was sweeping the beach, only to wake up and realize... that I was.

This made unexpected visits from friends an exceedingly embarrassing affair. I had come to dread the visits of once-welcomed friends for their pitiful, sympathetic, sometimes judgmental eyes roamed my house freely.

If you have friends that you like to go bless and visit, just send them a heads-up call first.

A huge expense of diapers blotted out a large portion of budget and my hands were practically sewed to the changing table as we often had an assembly line of up to three babies in diapers at once, four at the most. I better have a world record somewhere.

But once I dedicated my undivided attention and heart, without expecting anyone to rescue me... Without help, without murmuring poisoning my mind or bitterness souring my heart… That is when I saw mind-blowing favor and blessings kiss my feet wherever I walked. Favor dripped from my words and went out before me.

There are laws of life that say, "You reap what you sow," and "For every action there is a counter reaction."

The bin of flour was not used up, nor did the jar of oil run dry, according to the word of the LORD which He spoke by Elijah.

A clever way to bend this law, to shift the universe in your favor, is purely by sowing a diligent, cheerful attitude in your home. That tactic has opened up incredible opportunities for me.

I saw myself as raising nations. I chose to serve as if I was raising the next President or President's wife, CEO, engineer, or minister who would influence and help the next generation.

Are You Ruling or Being Ruled?

We were so poor we used old clothes for toilet paper. Yep!

Let me explain.

There was totally a cool wave of recycled, hippie ideas… Don't you just love those ideas? They come and go… really fast.

We wore hand-me-downs, and when we were through with them I couldn't donate them—no one would want to wear them! But I didn't want to waste them. So I cut them up and we used them for toilet paper.

Side note: it's taken me five years to un-train them that the toilet paper goes in the toilet, not the trash can.

So. Tell me. How does someone go from using t-shirts for toilet paper to an internationally-run online business worldwide, in a home business that she works once a month?

How does a woman go from filing divorce, fighting over her children at the police station, to… actually thriving in her marriage, taking refreshing retreats every few months, and going on date nights on a weekly basis?

> It comes down to this Law: She who is faithful with her territory will be given much more playground space.

I never DREAMED that by pursuing the very simplest of principles of service in thankfulness, that I'd get everything that my heart desired in return.

It comes down to this Law: She who is faithful with her territory will be given much more playground space.

You may feel like you have so little to work with. Your clothes are rags and you barely have two minutes to call "your own" in a laboriously active day of diaper changes, errands, and feeding mouths.

But over and over I have seen that when you are willing to be loyal with the territory that you inherited, it is the Lord Yahweh's delight to lavish us with more than what exists in the boundaries of our minds… *IN the land of the living, right NOW.*

"I remain confident of this: I will see the goodness of the Lord in the land of the living." (Psalms 27:13)

You couldn't stop the coming blessings even if you tried. They are the solid aftermath of your actions.

You have the same 24 hours as everyone else.

And guess what?

You can change the world with that.

"All you need is love, trust, and pixie dust." — quote from my daughter Kinsey… who reads a lot of a fairytales and books in general.

Learn to become a ruler, a Queen, over your kingdom—your time—and watch what will happen with your loyalty.

Smoke and Mirrors

Other people might come into your life and say you're not being faithful with your home, your life, your children, and your body. But it's not about them and what they perceive.

There was a time that I lived in a really tiny house. We had three children and had one closet for all three of them, one room for all three of them.

Everything was just wall-to-wall, furniture touching furniture. Everything I owned was orderly, but in such an enclosed tiny space it looked claustrophobic.

> I limited myself to one meeting outside the home per month.

I had a well-meaning friend come over and tell me that "God isn't going to give you anything more if you don't take care of what you have."

And as that sentence just fell on top of me, I gazed at him in complete despair under that heavy condemnation. He had no idea how hard I tried to keep things looking nice.

He did not know.

But God knew.

God knows you, He knows your heart, and the riddles and struggles in your life. He made a covenant between you and Him.

Creating Time for Business Out of Thin Air

How did I find time to work my business?

I limited myself to one meeting outside the home per month.

That was the commitment level I could give without straining my body and my relationships. My kids held me accountable as my personal enforcers because they liked me at home, but they are also my biggest teammates and want me to succeed.

But because I honored my family and managed my home well, I was very powerful when I did go out to work.

I limited activities and errands to Thursdays and Fridays, and we worked diligently in the mornings to get school done so I had time in the afternoons to invest in my business.

Or take naps… when the process of baking a human was happening.

This created beautiful pressure to get a large amount of work done in a short time.

It taught me to be productive because I had no time to waste.

I was very selective with my time and chose to only work with those who showed they were serious by attending trainings and our company's yearly convention.

This created beautiful pressure to get a large amount of work done in a short time.

They needed to be investing in themselves for me to invest in them.

Just like with my kids, I expected my team to grow up and become great, so I spoke life over them and taught them the principles I've shared with you in this book.

BONUS TIME-SAVER

Delegate to celebrate.

For a family to run smoothly, delegation, systems, and regular team meetings are essential.

I literally have one child whose job is to celebrate birthdays. That's her job.

I'm not a party person. I have so much on my plate, that's just one thing that I'm not very good at yet. But she's naturally gifted at making someone feel special on their special day. So I give her a budget and what she needs to celebrate the parties, and it gets done! That's her job in our family.

Running my home like a business absolutely revolutionized

Delegate to celebrate.

my life and gave me a sturdy, supportive foundation on which to build a thriving business, with less time and effort than one would think possible.

Finishing Well

We have an evening routine we call "crunch time" where we spend 5-10 minutes getting the house back in order so we can wake up to a house that is ready for the day.

We usually spend some time together as a family in the evening. I love to read aloud, but some seasons I was too tired to string words together.

So I'd play 20 minutes of a sermon or a teaching and we'd all listen together, sleeping on the warmth of wisdom instead of counterproductive entertainment.

That was how we'd finish our day to jumpstart the next.

A 5-Letter Word

Honor.

Honor means prioritizing your family first.

You must keep your business within boundaries so your family doesn't feel like they are playing second fiddle to your work.

When I am working my business, I am intensely focused. And when I am in mommy mode, I don't let business distract me. I keep my phone in my office. It never comes out of my office unless I leave the house. This is a constant battle of protection of my territory. I also turn the sound off on my phone.

This goes for email too. I check it when it's the right time for ME rather than letting it interrupt my day.

This has been HUGE for me.

My phone does not tell me when I should or

should not stare at it just because a new notification popped up. *I* choose when I will use it.

I will not be mastered by Facebook.

I only check the two groups I manage. Unless I'm tagged in something I don't see it. And I really don't miss it. If I'm meant to see it, my Maker makes sure I do.

This is real freedom.

I am ruler of my moments. I don't let myself be controlled by something that doesn't have my best interest in mind.

Not only that, but I don't want my kids to remember me with my white, screen-lit face glued to the phone and a deaf ear turned to their cute, freckle-faced love.

You can listen to the gentle, quiet voice in your head, or you are going to get a really painful one in the form of your most important relationships suffering.

Your family will resent you if you don't keep them first. This is a good, growing lesson. I embrace it, I don't run from it.

The phone is the biggest temptation.

71

1) I don't bring my phone on date night.

2) I don't sleep with my phone

3) I leave my phone in my office.

Those three things are very hard to do. But if you can master those three skills, your life will change.

Your soul, your mind, and your life are like a kingdom. They must be ruled or they will be overrun with thieves of time, joy, and peace. It's time to kill those distractions and reclaim YOUR life to YOUR will.

Reclaim your throne. Be Queen of your soul.

YOUR BEAUTIFUL LIFE STARTS NOW

1) Be master of your phone. You tell it when you will or will not pay attention to it, and set boundaries on hours when you will be available or not.

2) Ask your spouse, kids, and teammates when they can spare you to work and ask them for accountability.

3) Date your spouse, weekly, and without distraction. Focus is the start of romance.

CHAPTER 4

DITCH MERCY, GET AN APPETITE

If you've been looking for an all-purpose wild card, this is it.

It does a number of things; it doesn't solve just one issue.

When I've hit any roadblock, frustration, or problem, and exasperation screws with my head, this has been my saving grace.

The only difference between you and the dreamy life flying just out of reach from you is what's between your two ears.

Let me be very clear.

You are only limited by the lines you have drawn yourself.

If you want to play inside new levels of success, you're going to have to break those lines in half and brush them aside, regardless of any second lazy thought.

You are capable of much more than you think. You are more resourceful. There is a magnate power written in the very cells of your body. You're stronger and more joyful than the despair spinning around in your head.

You are only limited by the lines you have drawn yourself.

You have this innate power whether you realize it or not. A common problem is that when you don't know you have it, it can distract, frustrate, and imprison you.

Gossip, division, and strife effectively squash and distract it. To counteract this, we have…

SECRET # 4
A MERCILESS APPETITE TO LEARN

You must take responsibility for your current results.

Ditch Mercy. Get An Appetite

Why?

Because if you don't take action, nothing will ever change.

So you have to remain teachable and always be strengthening your mind. You have to be willing to do whatever it takes to succeed and follow those who have been there and done it before you.

When I began my journey to live beautiful, I knew I needed help—lots of it.

Every area of my life was out of control or diseased, and the thought patterns that delivered me to that recurring place needed to be uprooted and replaced.

> Because if you don't take action, nothing will ever change.

The monthly or weekly training available to me in religious circles or conferences was not enough to sweep out the messy strife in my cluttered mind... strife that manifested itself in my relationships and health.

I needed to completely reprogram myself.

77

"As a man thinks in his heart, so is he." (Proverbs 23:7)

I decided not to wait for anyone else to do this for me.

I fully submersed myself in thoughts of truth in the hope of drowning out the voices of despair and failure. In the process, I re-trained my brain with truth and wisdom.

A self-made boot-camp for my mind.

I took all my "white space"—every chance I had— to listen to anything that would guide me, increase wisdom, and build my skills.

> I decided not to wait for anyone else to do this for me.

In just the few spare chances I had gotten so far, I had already seen this technique of learning inside the "whites spaces" work inside my career, and now I wanted to apply it to my family. And that's when things started to shift drastically.

Who tells you what a mom is? The media does.

And as far as I can see, the picture the media paints is not exactly the greatest role model for being a wife and mom.

I get it, life is hard. Nobody is perfect. But who's telling you what a good mom looks like?

I used an iPod to download educational audio recordings.

I listened in the shower, while putting on makeup, cleaning, driving—even sleeping and... going to the bathroom. Use every second!

I would walk 30 minutes daily and listen over and over again until I could say the scripts or content before the speaker could. I'd try to memorize it.

And my life began to transform into something I did not recognize, as I intentionally and carefully fashioned myself into MY role model, chasing the better version of myself.

Fashioning Your Role Model

Some call it the 'subconscious mind', for some it's their 'inner voice', others call it the 'spirit man'.

Whatever it is, it is the most influential, con-

trolling factor in your life. It never sleeps and is always programmable and listening!

> Whatever it is, it is the most influential, controlling factor in your life. It never sleeps and is always programmable and listening!

Yes, you can even 'program' your mind with truth while you sleep!

If you (or your husband) don't like to listen to talking during sleep, there's even a strategy for that! WholeTones.com has amazing, specially-created music that sends wholesome notes and frequencies into your mind while you sleep. My husband and I love this resource!

Fish Are Friends, Not (Food) Crabs

At the Asian market there were live crabs. They were trapped, yet there wasn't a lid on the bucket. They would climb up the side but as soon as they reached the top edge, another crab would claw at them and they would fall back down. It was an endless cycle of everyone trying to get out at the same time, pulling each other down.

Sometimes, the reason you can't get out of the frying pan is because the walls are too high, and the minute you get to the top, claws of other people's fear introduce you to the floor again.

It is vital that you are very selective with whom you surround yourself.

When dealing with relationships, you must learn to create a framework of what you will do and what you won't do so you're not a doormat.

I've seen too many people get hurt when out of balance, all in the name of love.

Decide what you will spend and what you won't spend. Create boundaries that allow a safe place to commune inside of, and minimize wounds of life before they even happen.

I asked God for divine friends who were on the same page as me, teachable and up-lifting, hungry for more. That year He uprooted ALL of the current friends in my life and brought me to a new place. We moved to a new town.

I was willing to be alone if that was required to

protect myself from collective back-tracking, but God answered my prayer and provided positive friends.

I was able to submerge myself in friendships with older women who I gleaned invaluable inspiration from, and if it weren't for them I don't know if I would've made it. They were always speaking life, truth, optimism, belief, and faith. This can be the hardest tip to follow, but once you make the choice to do what's best for your family, it is His delight to bless you with friends who bring adventure and freedom.

Adopt a Villain Mindset

In a sense, this entire book is a manual on how to be rebellious.

We are teaching you how to rebel against stereotypes, prejudices, gossip, division, bitterness, and toxic habits. Sounds fun doesn't it?

That's because it IS more fun.

Difficult and simple, takes patience, but way more fun. And it's less tiring.

In fact, when you find out exactly what type of life

these techniques lead you to, it's irresistible. You just can't help rebelling against the miserable status quo.

You are in the business of going rogue.

In the name of rebellion, here's one more thing you don't ever have to bow down to again…

Poverty.

Get out of your mind the need to take away from each other.

The need to drive sharp bargains, cheat, beg, take, manipulate, or lust.

The gospel truth is that if you help others to grow and blossom, without check, without second thoughts, without stomping on their small progress, without ulterior motives, freely… then you will grow further than you thought possible.

By generously, richly adding to the lives around you, you can now create.

For example, we needed a bigger car. We outgrew ours.

So we started to create in our minds the perfect van.

We picked out the color and the cool gadgets that we wanted it to have, sunroof, and a CD player.

Every time we'd see a van we'd say, "Lord, thank you for our van," while blessing the family who had theirs. In gratefulness we would look out at the driveway and see if one had shown up yet. This was during our extremely painful budget years.

I drove a two-toned Honda—the hood was gold, the rest of the car was silver with no AC… *in the south y'all.*

"Unpleasant" is a nice, diplomatic term to describe it.

I had to limit driving it to only to the bare necessities. The girls would stop talking when they got too hot for the southern temperatures and having the windows rolled down just wasn't cutting it.

We held the image of our van with the most positive certainty that it was on its way to us.

Well… the ending of this story is that we didn't get a van.

But TWO.

That goes against everything anyone tells you… ever!!

I keep laughing about it. How rebellious is that?

Hang on. In case you didn't catch that, later on a new van, with our exact specifications was delivered on our driveway.

We came into agreement with a supreme power that said we were to be blessed and live prosperous lives, and that allowed the Lord to bring us the exact requested van. We created our van.

Hang on, I'm not done. This is so funny, watch.

> Jesus said, "It is the Father's pleasure to give you the Kingdom."

We needed Christmas lights one year. A thing so simple yet so painfully embarrassing, we simply had no budget for this light luxury. Our immediate family was distant so our family had to learn how to self-preserve, a mixed blessing.

So we, in our creative mind, we prayed for a Christmas tree and lights.

Two different families brought the tree and all sorts of lights and decorations.

Get definite with your requests.

Jesus said, "It is the Father's pleasure to give you the Kingdom."

"Anything is possible to those who believe."

"Whatsoever you ask for when you pray, believe that you receive them and you shall."

"I have come to you that you will live life and more abundantly." (Christa Version)

This is especially powerful in children. When my kid comes to me with a desire in their heart when they see a friend playing with something they want... I take the opportunity to teach them that, that kid took that toy from the warehouse in Heaven for them. It has their name on it.

But *you* have a warehouse full of toys and treasures with your name on it too. So when someone gets something that you want, you can actually look forward to the future with *joy* instead of with a spirit of competition because your warehouse is *full*. So choose to celebrate with your friend and celebrate their achievements.

This creates a huge amount of harmony and contentment.

This mindset that anything is possible and you can have all you desire for living a most abundant life is giving God the freedom to make it possible.

Why? Because He gave you free will. He can't legally act in your favor unless you legally release Him to.

The reverse is also true. The enemy can't legally act against you unless you legally release him to with your unchecked words.

Rise up out of competitive thoughts.

Supply is not limited. All the building posts have not been taken. No one has beat you to it.

Get rid of the poverty mindset and adopt a villain one.

Go rogue.

Find Out What Everyone Else is Doing and THEN—Don't do that

Game changer alert.

It's NOT always about what you're DOING but what you STOP doing.

If someone doesn't have the results you want in

your life, don't pattern your life after theirs! You have to be willing to limit the time you spend with them.

Because if they had the answers, they'd already have a million-dollar business with their results.

Here's the list of crabs we found in our life:

TV.

We don't do TV.

We don't listen to commercial radio or elsewhere.

Magazines.

> It's NOT always about what you're DOING but what you STOP doing.

We use a computer and internet if we want to watch a movie as a family. We don't waste any moments we could be filling with Scripture or worship music or other good stuff. I play Scripture all night long for my kids.

When The World Takes Your Hands and Hugs Away

I began playing Scripture when my fourth baby, Macy, was in the hospital.

She was 8 weeks old and only weighed about 6 pounds. She was on a ventilator and I wasn't allowed to hold her tiny form, I could only watch her. I felt so empty and helpless!

I thought there had to be something I could do for her, so I bought a CD player and I would play Scripture songs over her.

One that I gravitated to that was designed for playing over babies and helpless situations, is a work by Dennis Jernigan titled, "No Life Too Small."

The nurses kept turning it off. I'd always go and turn it back on.

When she got strong enough to come home, we kept the habit.

We have cheap CD players or remote speakers in every room and I bathe my kids in the Word night and day.

Even babies have a mind just as sharp, intelligent,

and powerful as a grown adult. Every mind is always hungry, always mercilessly soaking up information.

Control the information input, choose what comes back out of you and your children.

The person who rules the mind, rules the life. Don't let that person be Facebook, Instagram, TV, or the Media… let it be YOU.

Training Your Brain Resources

Song:

⤳ Dennis Jernigan—No Life Too Small

YouTube:

⤳ Danny Silk—Put Your Love On

⤳ WholeTones.com

Resources:

⤳ Dr. Norman Vincent Peale—Power of Positive Thinking

⤳ Dale Carnegie—How to Win Friends and Influence People

⤳ Chuck Black—The Kingdom Series

⤳ Frank E. Peretti—This Present Darkness/ Piercing the Darkness

⟿ lamplighter.net—Trusty the Train (for little kids) / Giant Killer (perfect for all ages)

TV show:

⟿ SidRoth.org

YOUR BEAUTIFUL LIFE STARTS NOW

1) Get a portable bluetooth speaker (water-proof!) so you can listen to truth anywhere and everywhere

2) Laminate Notecards of Life (affirmations, Scriptures, anything you want to drill into your mind…), scatter them around your home, in the shower, by the mirror, in the car, and in your purse.

CHAPTER 5

RIGHTEOUS MANIPULATION

Is there such a thing as righteous manipulation?

Let me ruffle your feathers a bit. There is.

Another, perhaps 'safer' term for this is 'negotiations.' That's all it is, basically. Selling some thing or selling an idea, through charming, clever influence and for the benefit of both parties.

Now. Simply put, your subconscious mind… is smart. And might be the block keep you from reaching further than you've ever reached before.

Because it is also protective of you.

But this can be counterproductive.

What it absolutely will NOT do is sacrifice your health, your time, or your peace of mind for the same success that you wish for. It will protect you from your own guilt and your own destruction in the best way it can. It will sabotage any efforts put forth to move forward with a wealthier lifestyle because you may have already shown that following the same path in a different way has cost you dearly.

So it's time to re-negotiate the terms of your success with your subconscious mind, on YOUR terms.

SECRET # 5
YOU WILL NOT COMPROMISE ON YOUR HEALTH

Try this out. Right now. Literally speak to your subconscious mind, thank it for protecting you, for being good to you, and thank it for serving you. Then say to yourself that you don't have to protect yourself in the same way anymore because this time, you will not compromise on your family, relationships, or your health. And be faithful to your words.

Release your subconscious mind from the walls it's built up against moving forward and let those walls crumble, because you have set guidelines for your time so that you can grow in a healthy way.

You've gotten picky, pricey, and selective with

your time, so now you are efficient and uncompromising.

Sweet Tip: Mornings Are Yours

Wouldn't it be nice having a guarantee that even if the zombie apocalypse happened tomorrow, inside your mind you'd be a fortress of peace and remain unaffected by the world's idea of a trying day??

Rocking your morning will set your whole day up for that type of peace of mind.

I know it's not always possible to have time to yourself first thing in the morning, especially if you have a new baby, illness, are moving, caring for an elder parent… just the seasons that life brings you. But the faster you can focus on YOU in the morning, the better everything flows.

If you start the day with the right mindset, it will help your kids to focus as well.

"The Miracle Morning" book by Hal Elrod is the bomb dot com. The morning routine he lays out in that book is the traitor to despairing days. You can learn more about this amazing morning routine on YouTube, but I really love the book. It teaches you how to really maximize your day.

I have customized it to my needs and my pace, and I don't do it every day—but as I am able. My goal is to get up at 5 am. I take Wednesdays and Saturdays off, and I don't force this schedule when we are traveling.

> This morning time is when I get my attitude right, so that whatever the day throws at me, I can smile, easily.

It's all about seasons. You have to do what's best for you and your family in each season you are in. As moms, our seasons, and our shoes, change so fast! The key is to steward the one you are in well.

I don't touch my phone or computer until my Miracle Morning is done.

If I am struggling or I don't like what I see in my home, it's 100% me. I have to take responsibility and be willing to continually work on me.

This morning time is when I get my attitude right, so that whatever the day throws at me, I can smile, easily.

Life can be difficult, and when there are times where there is nothing inside of me left to give, even an innocent question from my husband or child could cause a meltdown. But if I seize my mornings for myself, then I can give of myself fully again. I can give my children hugs and be gracious because I've already been refreshed.

You cannot give what you do not have.

Exercise is a key part of the Miracle Morning and to mommy success. I always have more energy on the days I work out.

When my kids were little and Jason wasn't working at home, my one activity a day consisted of piling them into the van and heading to the YMCA.

In the particular season I'm in now, I'm able to leave my little ones with my older girls and I get out of the house. But when I was unable to do that, I got us a Bellicon rebounder—a mini trampoline. It's very effective for lymphatic release and cardio, and it's also a lot of fun. My kids and I all do it so it's good for everyone.

> You cannot give what you do not have.

97

If you're homeschooling, building a business, and working on your marriage and being there for your kids, it's absolutely necessary that you exercise. Walk, run, rebound—do something to help you feel your best.

> The better you feel the more productive you are.

Here's the reality. You can go 3 times a week to physical therapy after your hips have been re-placed when you're older, OR you can exercise 3 times a week on YOUR terms and sustain the energy to play with your grandchildren when they are given to you, and sleep without any aches.

The better you feel the more productive you are.

I really work to protect our mornings. I don't schedule appointments or outings before noon. We get a ton of focused work done on the mornings we are home.

I am so much more productive when I get up early. But that makes for a really long day! So, my other secret is rest and read time. We always have rest time in the afternoon, no matter what age. Everyone must rest or read. They sit on their beds quietly, self-contained, reading or listening to some-thing, and many of them fall asleep.

This is my survival secret still to this day!

Rest is a Non-Negotiable

They say… "You can sleep when you're dead." Yeah, who is 'they'?

We think we can go, go, go every day from 8-5, yet everything else in this world is seasonal—why not us?

Give yourself grace to be human.

You have to submit to the seasons.

For instance, we had seasons of rest around each baby. I would take 6 months off my business each time I had a baby. Making a human is a lot of work and adjusting to a new baby is a huge transition.

We do take a rest day each week, but it's hard to feel rested any day when you have 4 in diapers.

Give yourself grace to be human.

When our business grew to the point where we

could afford it, we 'bought' our day of rest by getting take-out. We'd get a 200-count tray of nuggets from Chik-Fil-A and we'd eat it all day. That's how I got a day off.

When the Smiths brought another human into the world, we went into seed-planting mode.

No outside commitments or activities for my kids, unless they could get a ride from someone else. (There were a couple helpful friends who instrumentally helped… I'm looking at you two, Beth Gould and Denae King. So pray for a Gould and a King… a good king. Haha. Get it? Play on words.)

Once we had rested, recovered, and adjusted, we'd have a family meeting to decide what we wanted to learn next and then we'd do that one thing.

We chose activities we could do together so we could have similar schedules, and we didn't do more than one.

So, we all learned karate one year, took band another, ballet another…

That helped tremendously with my schedule.

Protect yourself, protect your family in every season. Release your subconscious mind of this

worry and loyally guard your life with grace for the seasons.

The Pot of Gold or Rather… the Pot of Energy—Same Thing

At the end of the rainbow is this thing called fasting.

Despite much controversy on the subject, I believe fasting is beneficial and in the Bible for a reason. I just choose to follow the instructions.

When I was not making a human, I would fast once a week.

This purified and detoxified my body. The end results look like multiplied energy, disappearing skin impurities, banishing foggy-brain, clear vision, passionate motivation, and all of this directly influenced my confidence and joy… which in turn improved relationships, sales, and harmony!! Hands up, coolest thing ever.

But it was a skill I built up to gradually.

Here's how I did it…

First, I said, there's no way I'm gonna fast food. I like food.

So we fasted TV for 5 days and when we turned it back on, we were completely awestruck at what we were putting into our mind and our spirit.

What we put into our mind will go into our heart. It deposits there, and out of the mouth the heart speaks. We had been putting so much junk into our hearts!

Fasting TV was huge, because I no longer was listening to commercials that were trying to sell me on a lifestyle I didn't want!

Ever heard of something along the lines of, "Hey, try this migraine medicine. It might make you lose sanity, make your boobs fall off, SLIGHT chance of death, and you'll never sleep again. But hey! You'll have a 24% chance of getting rid of your migraine!"

Yeah. What a bargain! But I prefer my boobs attached to myself, or something along those lines… Thanks though.

That stopped going in, so my subconscious was no longer getting contrary information about what I wanted my life to look like.

None of the shows we watched supported marriage, purity, or the mindset we wanted to have, so we never replaced any broken TVs, and now we don't own one at all. However our RVs have them. They were built-in, not my choice.

Next, I felt very strongly to fast the radio.

That was really hard.

I was a huge fan of music. I was a cheerleader and a hip-hopper and I loved to rock out to anything on the radio. But the music that I was listening to was spreading thoughts of heartache, death, depression, and anxiety over me. I didn't want the affairs, the broken families, or the depression described in so many songs. But that's what I was feeding my subconscious mind. So I had to stop doing radio.

That stopped going in, so my subconscious was no longer getting contrary information about what I wanted my life to look like.

As I built up this skill, now I was ready for fasting food.

And that was really hard because I didn't believe I could actually fast food, so here's how I did it.

I started with just one meal a week, and I did this for a few weeks.

> We can't do ANYTHING unless we are healthy. You can have everything you desire, but if you don't have health, it will mean nothing.

To be able to fast two meals, I spread it out over two separate days. I skipped dinner on the first day and then breakfast the second day and did not eat till noon.

Then I was able to skip 3 meals in the span of two days. I skipped lunch and dinner day one and breakfast day two.

Finally I was able to accomplish a full 24-hour fast.

I did this once a week if I wasn't nursing or pregnant.

I believe this is what allowed my body to repair

itself from the rigors of making humans, and I was able to run circles around my own kids.

When you are as far out of balance as I was, making humans every 14 months, it can take drastic measures to bring you back into balance.

The more mature I became, the more I realized that I simply had to make a strong commitment to my health.

I love life and I don't want to have my life compromised by having even one hour of dysfunction caused by sickness or headaches or other things people struggle with all the time.

We can't do ANYTHING unless we are healthy. You can have everything you desire, but if you don't have health, it will mean nothing.

My family and my business needed me to be my best physically.

Fasting once a week weaned me off being controlled by food and its emotional prison. I became my own master again.

We have fasted a lot. I have fasted up to 10 days, and my husband Jason has done a 40-day fast. Our marriage is a miracle. Our children are miracles—

we were done at one. And at three. And four. We almost lost number twelve.

I was in a major accident when I was pregnant with number thirteen (we literally named her "Miracle".) Over and over our life and our family have defied the odds and survived—even thrived. We didn't expect so much fruit, we just obeyed, and now our whole life is a miracle.

This is a powerful story, but who's to say it's the result of fasting? I don't know. All I know is that I enjoy testing out the unconventional ideas.

The Name of the Axe

There is a block that I have never seen even one human escape from. It is a trap that can snag us and keep us from thriving inside a playfully thrilling life. You have to chop it down. Thankfully we have just the thing.

The name of the axe is mercy.

We cannot overlook the importance and power of mercy.

In fact, I have learned that this is something known warriors and millionaires do daily.

"I can't hear love 'cause we're at war

"And revenge is so loud and the drums are so proud

"But oh, I'm in a cage and I hear mercy say, 'I'm here now.'

"And it's the only way out."

Andra Day, The Only Way Out.
A Soundtrack from the movie Ben Hur, 2016.

Mercy happens when you separate the action from the person who knifed you. Realizing that

The name of the axe is mercy.

whether they meant it or not, whether they're right or not, there was a series of events, thoughts, and lies that led up to that point.

Behind every action of harmful intention is a history that we'll never see.

Most of the time it isn't even about you.

Mercy is recognizing the full picture and letting go of your share in the trauma and the lies. Why?

Because you can't get any higher with it on your shoulders. It's too heavy and you know it.

It means washing yourself of the bitterness weighing you down, constricting your chest, and blinding your eyes so that you can breathe, walk, and see freely and love that person, freely.

Do this in the full knowledge that there is a law that exists that generates seven-fold recompense for what was stolen from you within that relationship. Your time, missed time, the could-have-been time, the what-if time, the time that is gone and *the time that you mourn will be returned to you seven-fold.*

But you have to claim it, and you can't do that if all you're holding onto is the trauma and lies. You can only carry one.

It's as if you received a gym membership for a year, as a gift. It is paid for in full. But if you don't let go of your comfortable bed, the tempting morsels of food, walk into the gym, announce who you are and claim your rights, then your beach body is gone.

See, bitterness is comfortable to wallow in. It's easy to stay in bed and eat the poison it feeds you because it goes down smoothly. But it will bring you nothing but destruction and you WILL forfeit your health. You can do nothing without your health.

Just like a gym, mercy is something you exercise daily, not just once to see results. To walk **Most of the time it isn't even about you.** lighter, stronger and more gracefully powerful, it is an axe you walk around with.

Resentment focuses your gaze on the wound in your gut. If you keep poking at it and stirring it up, it will never heal enough so that you can look up again. God is so excited to show you new things of exhilarating freedom, but if you can't look up from the past you'll never see it.

Let go and *let Him heal you* so that when you look at the person who caused this inside of you, you don't see the damage anymore, you just see a new beginning of love and hope reviving inside each other. Hit the reset button. Start over.

Whether they join you in that new future is their choice, but at least you aren't staggering through the days anymore. You are upright and whole.

Speak that future over yourself, over that person; write down the sweet hope in scripture and set it on your mirror in the bathroom so that when you wake up you stare into that future of blessing, with them in mind, for them.

Mercy and repentance alike are solely about making a trade.

An unbreathable toxic life in exchange for wholeness again.

It isn't for the other person, it isn't even for God...

It is fully for you, so that you can rest.

I'm not a pastor, counselor, therapist, emotional healer... This is just what has worked for me.

Your Beautiful Life Starts Now

1) To get it all done, start scheduling time-blocks. Pick 3 things you need to get done today: 1 in your personal life, 1 in your business life, and 1 in your home. Just keep doing that and you will make it.

2) Pick one area of your life you'd like to see improve. Maybe it's drinking water instead of soda. Maybe it's starting to exercise, maybe it's starting to do date nights and then moving into doing weekly date nights, maybe it's putting an alarm on your phone to schedule time to hug your children or to remind yourself to eat or drink water. Maybe it's to stop yelling at your kids. Whatever it is, pick ONE thing in that area and make that one small change for 30 days. Don't worry if you miss it or fall back. This is a journey and it's full of grace. Let us encourage you in our WonderMom Facebook

group where there's lots of videos and posts to encourage you.

Spoiler Alert! Keep an eye out for our next book for our tips and tricks on building a home-based business.

Resources

∞→ "The Miracle Morning", Hal Elrod

∞→ Movie: Ben Hur 2016, Paramount Motion Picture

∞→ Song: The Only Way Out by Andra Day

∞→ Every song by King and Country

∞→ Bellicon, an exercise device like a rebounder. Fast, easy, and gets your blood pumping.

CHAPTER 6

PEPPERMINT

Let's go into the ever-growing world of essential oils.

Peppermint is one of the most famous oils there is. It does a great many things, but this next secret I'm about to share with you has an uncanny simi-larity with this famous oil.

> They both act as a magnifying agent to drive home all of the other tools at your disposal.

They both act as a magnifying agent to drive home all of the other tools at your disposal.

If nothing else is working very well or at all but

you're following the steps precisely, then try applying this peppermint power into the mixture and watch it shift and breathe life.

SECRET # 6
POWERFUL PEPPERMINT PRAYER

Who likes to beg?

Nobody? Good.

Cause that's not what prayer is.

It is a great many things, but begging isn't on the list.

The truth is. You are a soul, a spirit, a mind, and a body. Prayer is aligning yourself in all four aspects into agreement with God's idea of your life.

Prayer is reminding yourself of who you are.

Why is this important?

For example. If an eagle created another eagle but that baby eagle was sent to another place, grew up among chickens, programmed by chickens, taught by chickens, begins to think she is a chicken... then she wouldn't even have the vocabulary to fathom flying, so why would she try? Yet she was designed to.

If Elohim Adonai, King of Kings, made you, what is keeping you from 'flying'?

Well.

The chickens. A.k.a. the environment.

Don't make the chicken problems your problems.

Don't let their fears be your fears. Once you realize you have the authority of an eagle and know that you were designed like an eagle, you can now live like an eagle and do the things you've always dreamed about: the dreams that exist in the sky.

Don't let any human tell you that you can't.

Prayer is returning to who God says you are and agreeing with your destiny.

> Don't make the chicken problems your problems.

The point is the Bible told us that we would do even more than what Jesus did, yet nobody is walking around raising the dead, healing people, and shooting miracles out from their sleeve.

What's up?

Many times prayer is defined for us as an assembly of people, and then someone really special stands up and everyone else throws in a couple 'amens' and bobs their head in agreement. And we call begging and boasting prayer.

Don't get me wrong, there is a place for that type of really strong community.

All I know is, Jesus never did that.

He healed people in public, He socialized with them, He fed them, He served them, and He taught in public.

Prayer was a pure thing He did between just Him and His father.

I wonder if He was just infusing Himself, because He says, "I only do what the Father tells me."

It's a bit unconventional considering the upbringing I had myself in religious circles.

But I enjoy trying out the unconventional.

Reprogram for Peppermints

One of my favorite pastors, Dr. Clarice Fluitt,

taught me this secret to unconventional praying and praying all the time.

The point is, prayer isn't confined to schedules, it's a lifestyle.

So one of the ways I give myself over into undivided prayer is I let the very cells of my body talk too. When I close my eyes, when my heart beats, when I fill my lungs with air, when my fingers move with love for Him, it is with delight I commune with Him with everything inside of me.

I also keep White Angelica essential oil by Young Living in my makeup bag and I mentally put on the armor of God (Ephesians 6:10-19) as I anoint each part of my body: belly, head, chest, wrists...

Many times I will attach scriptures or affirmations to organs, according to the ever-changing seasons. If you have a certain issue that is a desire of your heart, use something you do, or go to daily to trigger that prayer... for instance the shower, changing diapers, stopping at stop signs, etc.

Doing dishes is an opportunity to pray over my family's health and provision. Laundry is a trigger to pray over every person in my home. When driving I carry declarations and prayer request cards with me to use my driving time to pray over my husband, children, myself, and my business.

When you're doing the dishes, you can thank the Lord that you have hands that work, running water, and food to feed your family, even if you don't know where the next meal is coming from.

They're called Trigger Prayers.

Many of these can be found later in this book.

For instance, when we change diapers, we pray purity and protection over that child and for their future spouse.

Whatever my pain point was, I would transform it into a trigger prayer, attaching it to something daily so I'd be sure to pray over it with intense focus—and with faith.

What does praying in faith look like?

It means praying for what you can't see; thanking Him for what He hasn't done yet. Knowing with this child-like belief that it is indeed done. Checking the driveway for your new car, checking the mailbox for your check… believing that it is finished.

That's praying in faith.

At one point we were so broke I had no towels, but I would go to my cabinet and I'd have this one little raggedy towel, and I'd say, "Thank You so much for all these towels. I don't have enough room for them!" I would pray a prayer of faith. "Thank you so much that they're coming in! So many towels and I don't even know where they're coming from! And they're so beautiful!"

So instead of looking at my cabinets and going, "Oh look, I have no food…," I began thanking God for the food He was going to provide. I would speak what I desired to see, instead of what I didn't yet have.

That's a faith prayer.

I would look in my mailbox and say, "Lord, You know we need money. I'm thanking You right now! Is it in here yet?" And one day we got an anonymous phone call.

They said, "Look in your mailbox," and hung up.

Jason went to look and found $1,000 in cash. He was overwhelmed. We'd been asking the Lord for help, and He answered.

We got the towels, too.

A package arrived from a friend's mother… It was full of many prayer requests. There were mugs and they were wrapped in—you guessed it—beautiful, blue towels.

Reality Check

I need to tell you something. I am a thief, a liar, a cheater, and an adulterer.

I know, I know… but believe me, I am.

So here's the deal. Have you ever stolen a paper clip? Or a pen? Or bubblegum or anything an inch tall?

Have you ever lied? You know, those little white lies?

Have you ever admired the opposite sex? Those cute magazines that are conveniently stationed in the check-out line at the store you go to every other day? And you thought to yourself, "Wow, he's cute!"

Well, according to the Bible you are a self-confessed thief, liar, and adulterer at heart.

We have only covered three of the great laws of the planet. Laws that are written in your heart, that's how you know it's wrong. Nobody tells you it's wrong, you know it.

One thing is for certain: we will never be perfect.

The perfects don't live on planet earth, even though some may think they do.

But the thing is, every choice you make has rippling consequences no matter how big or small, whether good or bad, there will always be repercussions.

When you get in trouble and get caught, you go to jail.

Once in jail, then you face a judge and he declares whether you go to jail forever or you get to go free.

There was a wealthy merchant who came upon a field and on surveying the field he found a rare, exquisite treasure. He then sold everything he had in order to purchase the field that had the rare gem it is so that He was the legal owner.

Many times we think that the merchant is us and we are to sell everything, sacrifice our lifestyle, and that could be one translation. However I like to look at it that the merchant is actually Jesus, the field is the world, and you are the rare, exquisite treasure.

He gave up His position in Heaven to have the legal right to be your defender in the courtroom of Heaven.

All because He knows your value: you are an exquisite gem.

Who is this? Who does that?

He is an embodiment of love itself; breather of life, creator of mountains. YHWH swells the oceans up or dries them to dust. He melts hearts of stone and speaks in tones of thunder and lightning.

The trees, rocks, and mountains tremble in worship. The flowers sing and clap in adoration and love. The sunset dances in unparalleled energy just to please Him.

Yet His eyes are taken, stolen, by you.

You matter to Him.

God only knows what you've been through; God only knows how it's killing you. God only knows what they say about you. God sees your struggles, the pieces you keep trying to pick up… but there's a kind of love that God only knows.

We so often forget our position in Christ and the beauty of what He has done for us. Remember.

This is what communion is about.

Remember Him and His great sacrifice to ransom you, *all* your messes you have made and all the ones you will make.

I'd love to take communion every day but mostly before we go on a trip or before there's a big event or whenever my heart says, "It's time."

Yet His eyes are taken, stolen, by you.

We literally use whatever we have on hand—tortillas, or dried fruit… We grab whatever we can find for the 'bread', and we'll use our family's all-time favorite juice, Ninxgia Red by Young Living, or use water if we have to. We don't make it a huge act. I don't go to the store and consciously shop for that.

I just do my best and my best is good enough.

We ask the LORD to bless what we have, and we drink the juice in remembrance of His blood that was shed and thank Him.

We then take the tortilla and break it in pieces, reminding us of His broken body that carried all our sins, sickness, and brokenness. Our debt, paid in full, so we can be free. We do this to remind ourselves of His incredible sacrifice for us, and to act out our thanks to Him.

I actually say to my children all the time, "I have not arrived. I'm not perfect. I do not have all the answers and I don't expect you to have the answers. I love you and forgive you and I'm just asking you to do the same for me."

A powerful gift I can give my children is showing them that they don't have to be perfect, but there is forgiveness for everything that they do wrong today, in the past, and in the future.

My kids are very used to this outward confession and expression of gratitude. They know how to pray with me: "I thank you Lord for dying on the cross and for His sacrifice. I am forgiven, and I am redeemed, I am blessed, and I receive it today. Please help me walk in it and teach me to be all that I have been designed to be."

Taking communion shows my kids how to go to Him when I am not home and they are in a painful place. They know what to do and Who to go to. They know they have a living, breathing God who will never leave them or forsake them.

This has become more of a tradition to us than Christmas or Thanksgiving.

What a cool thing that my children will be doing this with their children someday.

Let the Quiet Speak

When something is in your heart, it is because it was put there by the Lord and it aligned with your destiny.

Even if people tell you it's impractical.

For instance, when I deeply desired a second child. There was fear because we did not have the finances, the resources, or the room. If another baby came, my husband would have to get really creative to find ways to support his family, and he'd be looking at the prospect of a third job.

I prayed, if we are not supposed to have another child, then take the desire out of my heart.

So I went to God and I told Him that I just wanted peace. Whatever it took.

Two days later my husband came to me saying he had peace about having another baby.

My heart stopped, my jaw dropped. I was afraid

to say anything because I thought he'd change his mind. I thought it was a fluke yet I got off birth-control and we were pregnant within the week.

Surrender your tender dreams that you're afraid to give voice to, stop being content to just fantasize about them, give them to the Lord and ask Him to move or take them out of your heart.

Marriage Wars

Really. I believed God could fix marriages.

But there was no way He could fix mine. Mine was the exception.

We went to counseling so I could gain more opinions and armies against my husband.

A pastor sat us down and asked, "Jason, do you want this marriage?" He is the one who gave a resounding "yes." The pastor looked at me, and I was the one who said, "Hell, no!"

Yes, it was me who wanted out.

But God asked me to give him six months. I laughed and said, "There is no way you can fix this, God. We are so past gone."

Then someone gave me a copy of the book, "The Power of a Praying Wife" by Stormie Omartian.

Now… I had been praying for my man and my marriage, but I had been praying all the wrong prayers.

I'd prayed for God to change my man. Fix him.

I hated him.

Sadly, I have to be real with you. I was that woman who asked God to remove my husband from this earth.

I didn't know that I was the one who needed to change. I thought I was doing everything I could possibly be doing right. By the way, even those wicked prayers I prayed, I still thought I was doing right because during those times of oppression I was suffocating.

Yet, I was desperate, so I read the book… every day for 30 days.

Every chapter ended with a prayer based on Scripture. I followed instructions and read the prayers over my husband even though I didn't feel like it. I was so ready to quit and leave.

But God's word does not return to Him void. It will accomplish what He sends it to do.

I found what changed, was me.

We've been married now for 23 years.

Praying the Word is powerful, because it allows you to pray specifically for big things, even when your emotions and faith are at an all-time low. Even when you don't see how things could improve, how God could provide, how healing could possibly come.

When you speak God's word over yourself and your family, supernatural power is released over your life.

A Customized Vow

How do you make a verse your own and pray it for your family?

I found what changed, was me.

It's easy—just insert your name, either last or first into the verse, or just say 'me'.

I believe this is the secret.

It's also important to say these prayers *out loud*. There's just a science to hearing your own voice declare goodness over your life and the lives of those you love.

Try it for 30 days.

Pray the scriptures daily and just see what He does for you and your family.

YOUR BEAUTIFUL LIFE STARTS NOW

1) Read "The Power of a Praying Wife" by Stormie Omartian

2) Commit to reading the prayers in this book out loud every day for 30 days. Keep them in your purse. Keep them in your bathroom. Read them in your car as you're waiting in traffic. Wherever you find idle space in your day.

3) Commit during shower time and bath time to filling your mind with positive and encouraging thoughts. You can start with SidRoth. org. Listening to Christian music radio is great, but that is what everyone else is doing. We want to do the opposite. Let's step it up a notch. We are training for a higher purpose and specialized mindset. We are training up our children to be the leaders of tomorrow.

4) Commit to speaking nothing negative out of your mouth and only speaking life over everyone you come into contact with for the next 30 days. This may be the most challenging assignment for you. I get it. But I believe you can do it.

CHAPTER 7

SMASH

Saving the best for last, I'd like to introduce my final secret… the big # 7…

SECRET # 7
SMASH

I don't know, all I know is that this… *this* is what brings in the stories.

Stories flooding on Facebook, letters, private messenger… On multiple platforms of social media, people are talking.

And they're talking about healing; about miracles. Impossible, painful walls crumbling like dust in their lives.

Let me explain…

There was a day early on in my journey where I really wanted the Lord to move quickly and powerfully in my life, and I realized I needed to take God at His word.

I'd been reading in Joshua 6 about the Israelites entering the promised land, only to face the walls of Jericho.

They were massive—13 feet high, 14 feet wide, built on a 30-foot slope, engineered for military defense.

But God told them not to touch it.

His battle plan looked humanly foolish. They were to march around the walls for six days, not saying a word.

And on the seventh day they were to march around it seven times, then they blew their trumpets, shouted, and the walls fell down.

When I read that, I thought, "Hey, I've got some walls in my life."

So I sat my kids down and looked in their eyes and said, "I want you to write down what you want God to do for you." I told them, "Ask God for anything."

And they asked, "Anything?" I said, "Let's pretend

Jesus is sitting right here in this empty chair, and let's ask him for ANYTHING." And their eyes grew big and with a catch in my throat I said, "Yes, anything you can ask, hope, dream, or imagine," all while wondering what the hell I was doing. But that's what the Bible had said, and I was choosing to believe it… because nothing else I was doing was working.

Meanwhile, I was stretching my own faith because at this point in our life, Jason

> But God told them not to touch it.

had maxed out the income he could make at his job. There was no more promotion for him. We both had college degrees but there was no way I could work, and we had a crippling amount of student-loan debts.

As our family continued to grow we were living on food stamps.

We qualified for every bit of state aid available. In fact, when we applied, they looked at the numbers and said, "How are you surviving?"

Sometimes Jason would eat only one tortilla a day.

Let me introduce you to a perfectly-created, paralyzing whirlpool called food stamps.

When you're on food stamps, you have to run further and harder in this rat-race, to double what you're bringing in, in order to trump the need and co-dependency of being on them. So to try to get off the system, you have to greatly increase your income. Yet you must report that increased income, and when that happens, they decrease your food stamps significantly or take you off completely, at a time when you're likely not completely self-sufficient on your own yet.

We wanted out of this trap... but that seemed impossible.

If you've ever been on food stamps, you know exactly what I'm talking about. If you' haven't, praise God you've never had to deal with this.

If you currently are on food stamps, I get it. There is a season and time for that. We needed it desperately. But when you want off to be self-sustaining, it can feel hopeless.

As younger mom of 12 at the time, I saw a commercial of a widely-accepted family dream vacation in America... to take your family to experience a magical place called Disneyland.

But then came the reality of how to get there, get inside, eat, airfare, hotel, and then turn around and get home without it decimating our monthly expenses and debt.

A deep longing of being a mom and dad is to watch their children enjoy life to the fullest, but when you can't fulfill that desire it's like taking a piece of your heart and killing it.

Something that happened every time a commercial came on or I scrolled through Facebook.

So I tearfully wrote down, "Take my family to Disneyland," without much belief.

We're talking $20,000 easily.

So, the kids and I all wrote stuff out and we didn't read it out loud.

It was very personal between me and the Lord and between them and God.

We stuck the requests in a bowl, and for six days we marched around it.

On the seventh day we marched around the bowl

on the table seven times and proudly blew our fake horns and screamed.

The scripture says you give us the desires of our hearts and I have nothing to lose… but I have everything to gain.

Then I stuck the bowl on a shelf and didn't look at it. But I knew we had stirred up a massive storm, triggering the kids and definitely started awakening a subtle anticipation.

> The scripture says you give us the desires of our hearts and I have nothing to lose... but I have everything to gain.

Two or three years later, a passing thought reminded me about the bowl.

So I pulled it down off the shelf and started to read some of the things we had written. And I was SHOCKED, mildly put, because most everything had been fulfilled, or recognized.

We had taken the kids to not JUST Disneyland, but also to Universal Studios, Islands of Adventure, Discovery Cove, Sea World, and the beach for 6 weeks.

- We had gotten off food stamps.
- We had payed down our debt.
- We had restored relationships.

All of these insurmountable, impenetrable, un-movable Jericho walls in our lives had been smashed to dust.

There was no way we could have done those things in our own strength. Only God.

I was horrified.

I had been talking to the almighty King of Kings, the Lord of Lords, the ruler of all, Whose ways are higher than mine. His words are still expanding the universe thousands of lightyears per second... and I had asked Him to get me off food stamps!

I SHOULD HAVE ASKED FOR MORE!!!

... like a housecleaner. (Who else needs one 24/7?)

Ask for BIG things and march around them in faith.

We did a trip recently and we didn't do our

marching thing, and halfway there I had two kids come to me and say, "Mom, we didn't march around the RV. We need to march!"

I nodded, but I just kind of shelved it.

> Ask for BIG things and march around them in faith.

Then, another couple of hours down the road, I hear Macy on the walkie-talkie—"Mom, your left tire's low," on a rig on a trailer that I was driving alone.

I pulled over and there were three huge bubbles on the tire!

It was such a mercy she spotted it because I didn't have Jason with me and we didn't need a blown tire!

We caught it just in time…. and we sort of had this surreal feeling of what could have happened.

Jericho In Life

We will also march around any new houses, new vehicles, places we go… This is our way of praying protection over us.

Again, we take the Jericho walls example and physically march around, asking for protection and angels to guide us and the Holy Spirit to speak to us and open our ears, eyes, and heart to be guided by Him on our journey.

Jericho isn't just a cool idea to mull over. Jericho was a symbol of deep fear and the manifestation of an unsettling, unattained desire. A block to a dream too big to handle alone.

Yet Jericho itself is a story of a people who gave their deep-seated and VERY VALID, VERY REAL problems, doubts, and fears to a God bigger than them, in faith.. and Jericho is a story of what has already happened.

We all know how that story ended.

In our WonderMom Facebook group, we have been marching around Jericho walls and in the last few months some amazing reports have come in proving that God is still in the business of smashing walls and moving mountains.

Try it out and join the stories.

Your Beautiful Life Starts Now

1) March around your Jericho—the "impossibles" in your life like your family, marriage, job, home, career, goals, cars… What we did, we wrote our deepest desires on a piece of paper. I invited my husband and children to do the same. We put them in a bowl or basket or box and physically marched around our written desires in prayer. We set them aside for about 2 years until I felt led to review them, and I was awestruck when I saw the Lord show himself so strong in my willingness to surrender. I can't wait to hear your Jericho testimonies. Be sure to post them in our WonderMom Facebook group.

2) Watch for our upcoming announcements for our next Jericho March where you send your Jericho walls to us through the WonderMom facebook group, we will collect them and

march around them as a family and return them to you.

Here's some stories that have been sent in. We're so very grateful to these ladies for sharing. Let's celebrate with them!

"Our walls are coming down!!!! Mental and emotional battles that were tormenting are now GONE!!! We are walking in the midst of a HUGE financial breakthrough - we are about to become mortgage-debt free!!!"

~ Megan Dale

"'I pray that my daughter is seizure-free and grows out of them'... I included that in my letter and we just celebrated her being 1 year with no seizures!!"

~ Nancy Gray Hansen

"My husband got a new job, relocating to a new state in a few months!!! Walls are falling off our marriage, my husband's job, direction for our future... We have checked off several of the requests for the past three months. Very specific prayers are being answered!

"My daughter said, 'Do you believe that

God will do those things you've asked him for?' My husband said, 'Yes, I believe,' and my daughter replied, 'Dad, then it's done!' and she walked away.

"All because we started marching around our home and asking God to break down the walls of Jericho in our lives!"

~ Lara Tugbiyele

"You have no idea what God will set into motion by one simple act of obedience!! Trust God. Trust the process. We desperately needed a great staff and shortly after we sent out our Jericho letters we had an amazingly talented stylist apply and the best ray-of-sunshine front desk coordinator apply! My husband also started a new job paying a lot more! When Christa said, 'Don't hold back when asking God for what you want,' well I didn't! And I can't wait to see what he continues to do!!!"

~ Tiffany Ortega

Wait! I have one more thing...

I learned from friends who do emotional releasing, along with a program called *Dynamic Neural*

144

Retraining, that a lot of times our mind, will, and emotions hit walls because of an overactive limbic system and/or due to past traumas. If you suffer from any of the following issues: fatigue, pain, irritable bowel syndrome, hypersensitivity, chemical and food sensitivities, energy issues, anxiety, inflammation, or a wide range of other physical issues, then you may wish to focus on this prayer for 30 days. The goal is to bring harmony and balance to the body, soul, and spirit so we can run faster.

Each person is made up of a spirit, soul, and body. To clarify, the soul is the mind, will, and emotions.

What I learned from my friends, we came up with this prayer. For the sake of this prayer, when we say "I" or "you", we mean "spirit, soul, and body".

> *Spirit, soul, and body, you have carried so much and have been working overtime for far too long. You've been sending my body false messages in the form of various health issues. These symptoms are a result of cross wiring in my limbic system, and these over-reactive and over-protective mechanisms have caused me to isolate and withdraw. This is an old, outdated pattern,*

and I know that you were only trying to protect me.

But now it's time for a new pattern. I command for a disconnect. I choose to forgive, and bless, and release you. I choose now to rewire you for you have done nothing wrong.

From today forward, we choose to forgive, bless, and release each other.

I love you "self." You are the best self ever. I am so proud of you! Thank you for protecting me the best way you know how!! I know you didn't have all the information and you have been working overtime. But you can relax now. We have a new program that we are running. I choose to be comfortable and at ease in any social situation. I am capable and calm in any situation. I am healthy and strong. I communicate with ease and grace. I am. I know. I feel. I find. I see. I am full of vitality, and I love my life!! I can do all things through Christ who gives me strength. I have Wisdom. I step into my higher self. I am non-judgmental and full of love. I believe life is great. I am coura-

geous. I am forgiven and I forgive. I give up hopelessness. I do not compare. I celebrate others. I am positive. I have joy in my life.

Congratulations self. I am so happy for you. This is a fantastic step forward and is exactly what you need to change your life. I am so proud of you. Thank you to my family for our best years are ahead of us.

With that in mind these are the prayers I pray over my family. I cover my family with the word daily. You can do the same: just insert your own name in place of "Smith" to use them for your family! You can insert your last name, or spouse, or children, or all of the above... I have always trusted GOD knows my heart and I like to say "the Smiths" to cover us all.

Prayers of protection that were sent to me and that I've adopted:

This is one sent to me from my friend Harvey Jensen. (Everybody loves Harvey!) I use this as my 'emergency' prayer, any time I feel unsettled. You can put this one in your notes on your phone so you can pull it up anytime you need:

Father, I thank you for today. I invite you into the midst of this Lord. I bind, silence, and remove every demon, every unclean spirit, every familiar spirit, and every fallen angel out of here in Jesus' name. I forbid any human spirits from channeling, translating, or astral projecting in or out of the atmosphere. Lord, please post your angels around me/us and allow the 7 spirits of God to flow freely in this place. Lord Jesus, I invite you into this place right now, I declare your Lordship over this place and over this time, and I give you thanks in advance for what you are about to do. In Jesus' name. Amen.

This is from my friend Heather Portwood who does a lot of research and runs an educational YouTube channel on how frequencies and electricity affect the way we think and respond. Thank you, Heather, for your forefront movement enlightening us!

Dear Heavenly Father, I bind and block all sources of energy attacking me and my family, by the blood of Yeshua. I bind weaponized electromagnetic frequency, light, sound, heat, and slow and fast wave-

lengths, and decree... you are neutralized and ineffective over, though, and around me and my family.

I set a gold faraday cage as a protective barrier around me and my family, any seen and unseen, known and unknown receivers, this includes implants, electrodes, planted devices, and foreign DNA that is in my body and my family's bodies. I disallow any sent signals to reach their intended targets, including binding all signals from satellites and algorithms. I place a keyhole blocker, from the inside, in every cell of my body, which disallows all weaponized energies to reach their intended destinations, by the power and the blood in the name of Jesus. I quell anxious tension in my body. I make no alignment with fear. I call and decree alignment with courage over myself and my family. I set gold as a protective barrier around my limbic system. I disallow fear or tension to fuel energy in the atmosphere meant for harm or evil purposes. I decree acceptance of myself and my family through the love and the sacrifice of Jesus. I am fearfully and wonderfully made! Amen.

Here are some proven verbiage I pray over my family. Where I say "Smith", insert your name.

- ∞⟶ YOU will cause the Smiths to become the father of a great nation. YOU will bless me/us and make my/our name famous, and the Smiths will be a blessing to many others. (Genesis 12:1 TLB) (This is why we call our children "nations".)

- ∞⟶ YOU will bless those who bless us and curse those who curse me/us; and the entire world will be blessed because of us. (Genesis 12:3 TLB)

- ∞⟶ Be delighted with the LORD. Then he will give (the Smiths) the desires of our hearts. Commit everything (the Smiths) do to the LORD, and He will act. We trust HIM to help us/me. (Psalm 37:4-5)

- ∞⟶ My sons will someday be kings like their father. They shall sit on thrones around the world! (Psalm 45:16 TLB)

- ∞⟶ God is (the Smiths') refuge and strength, a tested help in times of trouble. And so we need not fear even if the world blows up and the mountains crumble into the sea. (Psalm 46:1 TLB)

∞→ (The Smiths) live in the shadow of the almighty El Shaddai, sheltered by my GOD who is above all gods. HE alone is MY refuge; my place of safety. He is my GOD and I am trusting HIM. He rescues me from every trap and protects me from the fatal plague. He will shield me with His wings! They will shelter me. HIS faithful promises are my armor. No I don't need to be afraid of the dark any more, nor fear the dangers of the day, nor dread the plagues of darkness, nor disaster in the morning. (Psalm 91 TLB)

∞→ He fills me with strength and protects me wherever I go. (Psalm 18:32 TLB)

∞→ But as for me, my contentment is not in wealth but in seeing You. When I awaken, I will be fully satisfied, for I will see you face to face. (Psalm 17:15 TLB)

∞→ Some nations boast of armies and weaponry, but our boast is in the LORD our GOD. (Psalm 20:7 TLB)

∞→ I am expecting the LORD to rescue me again, so that once again I will see His goodness to me here in the land of the living. (Psalm 27:13 TLB)

∽→ I will not be impatient. I wait for the LORD and He will come and save me! I will be brave, stouthearted, and courageous. Yes, wait and HE will help me. (Psalm 27:14 TLB)

∽→ Assign (the Smiths') Godliness and Integrity as my bodyguards, for I expect you to protect me and to ransom me from all my troubles. (Psalm 24:21 TLB)

∽→ God's word that goes out of (the Smith's) mouth will not return to us empty but will accomplish what HE desires and will achieve the purpose in our life for which HE sent it. (Isaiah 55:11 NKJ)

∽→ As we go, GOD will be with (the Smith's) mouths and teach us what we are to say. (Exodus 4:12 NKJ)

∽→ The LORD will perfect that which concerns (the Smiths). (Psalm 138:8 NKJ)

∽→ I praise you that (the Smiths) are fearfully and wonderfully made. (Psalm 139:14 NKJ)

∽→ The peace of GOD that surpasses all understanding guards (the Smith's) heart and mind through Christ Jesus. (Philippians 4:7 NKJ)

∽→ (The Smith's) steps are ordered by the LORD and HE delights in my way. (Psalm 37:23 NKJ)

- ⟿ Do not forsake the works of (the Smith's) hands. (Psalm 138:8 NKJ)

- ⟿ The LORD establishes the work of (the Smith's) hands. (Psalm 90:17 NKJ)

- ⟿ (The Smiths) commits our works to the LORD and OUR thoughts are established. (Proverbs 16:3 NKJ)

- ⟿ As (the Smiths) go, God will be with our mouth and teach us what to say. (Exodus 4:12 NKJ)

- ⟿ (The Smiths) is swift to hear, slow to speak, and slow to anger. (James 1:19 JASB)

- ⟿ Wealth and riches will be in (the Smith's) house because we are generous and full of compassion and righteousness." (Psalm 112:3-4 NKJ)

- ⟿ That the God of our Lord Jesus Christ, the Father of glory, may give to ("the Smiths) the spirit of wisdom and revelation in the knowledge of Him, the eyes of our understanding being enlightened; that we may know what is the hope of His calling, what are the riches of the glory of His inheritance in the saints. (Ephesians 1:17-18 KJV)

∞⟶ The fruits of the Spirit are evident in (the Smith's) life: Love, joy, peace, patience, kindness, goodness, faithfulness, gentleness, and self-control. (Galatians 5:22 NKJ)

When all else fails and you don't know what else to do, just pray this one; it is all-encompassing:

When I sit enthroned under the shadow of Shaddai, I am hidden in the strength of God Most High. He's the hope that holds me and the Stronghold to shelter me, the only God for me, and my great confidence. He will rescue me from every hidden trap of the enemy, and he will protect me from false accusation and any deadly curse. His massive arms are wrapped around me, protecting me. I can run under his covering of majesty and hide. His arms of faithfulness are a shield keeping me from harm. I will never worry about an attack of demonic forces at night nor have to fear a spirit of darkness coming against me. Don't fear a thing! Whether by night or by day, demonic danger will not trouble (the Smith's). Nor will the powers of evil launch against (the Smith's). Even in time of disaster with thousands and thousands being killed, we will remain unscathed and unharmed. We will be a spectator as the wicked perish in judgment. For they will be paid back for what they have done! When we live our lives within the shadow of God Most High, our secret hiding place, we will always be shielded from harm. How then can evil prevail against us or disease infect us? God sends angels with special orders to protect us wherever we go, defending us from all harm. If we walk into a trap, they'll be there for us and keep us from stumbling. We'll even walk unharmed among the fiercest powers of darkness, trampling every one of them beneath our feet! For here's what the Lord has spoken to me; "Because you have delighted in me as my great lover, I will greatly protect you. I will set you in a high place, safe and secure before my face. I will answer your cry for help every time you pray, and you will find and feel my presence even in your time of pressure and trouble. I will be your glorious hero and give you a feast. You will be satisfied with a full life and with all that I do for you. For you will enjoy the fullness of my salvation. (Psalm 91 PTL)

Prayers For Your Children

(The Smith's) children have…

⟶ My children have the hearing heart of Samuel (1 Samuel 3:2-18)

⟶ My child is like an OLIVE plant (Psalm 128:3)

⟶ (Sons) Vigorous and tall as growing plants (Psalm 144:12)

⟶ (Daughters) of graceful beauty like the pillars of a palace wall.

⟶ Is a child of Light (John 12:36)

⟶ Has the ordination of Jeremiah (Jeremiah 1:5-8)

⟶ Has David's understanding of God's authority (1 Samuel 24:6)

⟶ My sons and daughters arise* in one accord to extol her virtues,** and my husband arises to speak of me in glowing terms. (Proverbs 31:28 NKJ)
"arise" means to rise up in power
**"extol her virtues" means the children cheer, "Hooray, hooray for our mother!"*

⟶ My children follow God's ways. They won't walk in step with the wicked, nor share the sinner's way, nor be found sitting in the scorner's seat. My children's pleasure and passion is remaining true to the Word of "I Am," meditating day and night in the true revelation of light. They will be standing firm like a flourishing tree planted by God's design, deeply rooted by the brooks of bliss, bearing fruit in every season of their life. (Psalm 1:1-3 PTL)

⟶ My children are well taught by the LORD and great shall be their peace. (Isaiah 54:13 NKJ)

⟶ My children honor their father and mother which is the first commandment with promise that it may be well with them and they may live long on the earth. (Ephesians 6:2-3 NKJ)

Prayers For Your Husband

⟶ I pray for my husband to have the...

... Spirit of Truth (John 14:16)

... Wisdom of Solomon (1 Kings 3:28)

... Faith of Abraham (Hebrews 11:8-12)

... Grace of Noah (Genesis 6:8)

... Anointing of David (1 Samuel 16:12)

... Valor of Gideon (Judges 6:12)

... Courage of Joshua (Josh 1:18)

... Wholeheartedness of Caleb (Numbers 14:24)

- I submit myself unto my own husband as unto the LORD. For he is the head of me, even as Christ is the head of the church; and HE is the savior of the body. Therefore as the church is subject unto Christ, so let me be to my own husband in everything. (Ephesians 5:22-24)

- I pray that I may come to (my husband) with joy by the will of God, and may be refreshed together with him. (Romans 15:32)

- (My husband) loves me as Christ loves the church and gives himself up for me. (Ephesians 5:25)

- (My husband) finds me a virtuous wife, whose worth is far above rubies. His heart safely trusts me, so that he will have no lack of gain and I will do him good and no evil all the days of my life. (Proverbs 31:10-12 NKJ)

- (My husband) is known in the city when he sits among the elders of the land. (Proverbs 31:23 NKJ)

- I am (my husband's) and his desire is toward me. (Song of Solomon 7:10 NKJ)

- (My husband) dwells with me in understanding, giving me honor, and as being heirs together of the grace of life, so that his prayers are not hindered. (1 Peter 3:7 NKJ)

Prayers for Yourself

For me! I prayed this for myself, that I would have the…

> … Spiritual wealth of Anna (Luke 2:36, 38)
>
> … Faith of Rahab (Hebrews 11:31)
>
> … Beauty of Sarah (Genesis 12:11)
>
> … Courage of Rebekah (Genesis 24)
>
> … Strength of Deborah (Judges 4:4-16)
>
> … Commitment of Ruth (Ruth)
>
> … Clear Judgment of Esther (Esther)
>
> … Wisdom of Abigail (1 Samuel 25:1-42)
>
> … Purity of Mary (Luke 1,2)

I will be devoted to my husband even if he does not obey the Word of God. My kind conduct may win him over without me saying a thing. When he observes my pure, godly life before God, it will impact him deeply. Let my true beauty come from my inner personality, not a focus on the external. For lasting beauty comes from a gentle and peaceful spirit, which is precious in God's sight and is much more important than outward adornment. (1 Peter 3:1-4 PTL).

> I am a wise woman who builds up my house with my own hands. (Proverbs 14:1 NKJ)

> I shall be a fruitful vine in the very heart of my home. (Psalm 128:3 NKJ)

> For your royal bridegroom is ravished by my beautiful brightness. (Psalm 45:11 PTL)

BEFORE YOU GO...

In the name of being unconventional, not everything in here might be a perfect fit for you.

I hope you have taken the baby and left the bathwater.

I hope you've realized what is valuable, that you take it, use it, and leave the rest.

Don't be a follower.

That includes me. Don't follow me.

Follow your own results and research. I'm just sharing what has worked for me and if this blesses you, then I can't wait to hear your story.

Yes! Send me your testimony! Send it to our WonderMom Facebook community.

And if you know of anyone who is hungry, struggling, or hurting, why not give them the gift of a best friend?

There's multiple options and ways to do life, but you should know that there are inevitable laws that exist. I didn't make them up. They're just as true and in effect as the law of gravity. This book acknowledges these laws and shows you how to maneuver them in the easiest way so they're not working against you, but for you.

Feeling overwhelmed?

Pick two things.

Two points you found that soothed an extra sore place for you in your life and master those two things. Take 28 days to weave them into your life and watch the transformation take you to a softer place than before.

Lastly, I'm proud of you.

Of all the things I am most excited to hear is the success testament that starts the minute you close the last page.

You are a good wife and a good mama and that is the most queenly mantle that exists today. It is the most powerful position and the most honorable.

You have a platform that transforms both this generation and the next. Yes, the business of changing diapers and making bottles is the most honorable, because it is as if you are ministering to the Lord Himself.

Again, you just might be raising my future son/daughter-in-law so no pressure.

I want you to know that you came onto this earth fully capable to obtain the deepest desires of your heart. The quiet ones that you don't even give voice to out loud anymore.

Color your hair (naturally of COURSE...), try escargot (well, MAYBE), travel (yes, just... YES), jump out of a plane (take selfies cause I ain't gonna join you), have a new baby (MULTIPLY MAMA), promote up (Get it, Boss), and get unconventional.

Let's Be Best Friends

I would love to stay connected with you, Beautiful Friend!

Of all the things I am most excited to hear is the success testament that starts the minute you close the last page of this book. I can't wait to hear your story, like this one from Kayla:

Before reading Christa's book, I had diffi-culty focusing on what was most important in life. I was worried about how my kids would turn out, stressed about money, and over committing in an effort to look like everything was in control. Christa's words reached deep inside of me and brought heart back to life! She gave me oodles of clear, specific ways to transform my life and become the best me. Every woman needs to hear this life-giving message so she can change her life and live beautifully.

Join our WonderMom movement. We want to join hands with you here:

Subscribe to my YouTube Channel where I share more tips and secrets with you: "WonderMom"

Connect with me on Instagram: CHRISTASMITH_

Join our "WonderMom" Facebook group commu-nity with thousands of other like-minded friends!

Bookmark our website: LiveBeautifulBook.com

Prior to Christa's training and WonderMom, I was feeling like such a failure as a parent. I would go to bed at night with this heaviness and guilt that I was messing up my kids. I grew up as an only child and although I have a Doctorate, I was really clueless when it came to parenting and raising children. Using some specific resources Christa recommends and simple techniques and tools, Christa has helped me act and feel like a GOOD PARENT. My 5- and 8-year old children and I have deeper, more loving connections, smoother non-chaotic days, and I go to bed at night feeling and knowing I AM A GOOD MOM and I am ENOUGH!

I am so grateful to Christa and all she pours out into us WONDERMOMS!

Mary Starr Carter

Christa's community has blessed me tremendously! I have learned practical ways to groom our children for success and together as a family, we have all been consistently practicing the skills she teaches. Last year, listening to a talk Christa gave about having a "vision bowl" and walking around your "Jericho," I'm so stinking excited to say that we have consistently put this tool into practice in our home. God has answered so many prayers for us as a result, including my husband getting a new job. We will be relocating in two weeks, selling our house three weeks before we move. We marched around our house several times! Oh my goodness, I could go on for days what learning from Christa has done from us. Thank you so much for being a vessel! We are truly grateful!

Lara Tugbiyele

I look forward to continuously learning from Christa, and my kids love implementing what they learn from her as well. Christa's kind, loving, and wise spirit always encourages me to be a better mom and gives me the skills and practical tips I need to do so! My friends love learning from her too and we all discuss what we learn and how well it's working on our children. Thank you Christa!

Brittany Howell

Three and half years ago Christa did a business training call with my team and mentioned some specific resources that might help. We read one of the books out loud to our younger kids and attended some other training she recommended that was life-changing!

From what we learned and because of Christa's influence, we changed churches and got spirit-filled. One of my daughters married one of the pastors and she's now in ministry too. A second daughter is in her 2nd year at Bethel and she is very powerfully prophetic. One of my sons is at another school similar to Bethel and will very likely become a pastor as he is a very prophetic intercessor. Another of my daughters is succeeding at her job because of the training Christa recommended. And daughter will be attending Bethel next year. Another son is slowly returning to our family because of tools Christa recommended as well as sozo and inner healing.

My hubby and I are so much closer and getting freer every day. And I realized I needed to step back and regroup from being a workaholic and realizing I would be losing my family if I continued on in this journey that was way out of balance.

My hubby and I have been invited to be in leadership at our church, we've been trained in sozo, and now we are leading a home group that God seems to be blessing.

This is a short synopsis of just some of the amazing growth our family has experienced, all because Christa was willing to offer her time to serve our team when she didn't stand to benefit whatsoever in doing so.

It's still amazing to see how one act of service and God multiplying her teaching can transform a whole family.

Whenever we share our testimony, these are some of the bullet points we mention of how God worked miraculously in our family. Old friends don't recognize us. Christa, I've said it before and I'll say it again – thank you!

Sharon Koehn

Made in the USA
San Bernardino, CA
04 July 2019